William Faulkner, Gavin Stevens, and the Cavalier Tradition

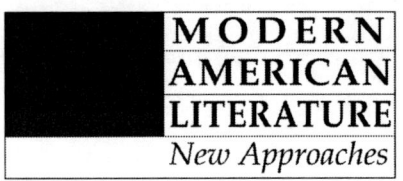

Yoshinobu Hakutani
General Editor

Vol. 58

PETER LANG
New York • Washington, D.C./Baltimore • Bern
Frankfurt • Berlin • Brussels • Vienna • Oxford

Lorie Watkins Fulton

William Faulkner, Gavin Stevens, and the Cavalier Tradition

Dear Claude,
Thanks for all of your help with this. You're next!
Lori

PETER LANG
New York • Washington, D.C./Baltimore • Bern
Frankfurt • Berlin • Brussels • Vienna • Oxford

Library of Congress Cataloging-in-Publication Data

Fulton, Lorie Watkins.
William Faulkner, Gavin Stevens, and the Cavalier tradition /
Lorie Watkins Fulton.
p. cm. — (Modern American literature: new approaches; v. 58)
Includes bibliographical references and index.
1. Faulkner, William, 1897–1962—Criticism
and interpretation. I. Title.
PS3511.A86Z78328   813'.52—dc22   2010023355
ISBN 978-1-4331-1155-6
ISSN 1078-0521

Bibliographic information published by **Die Deutsche Nationalbibliothek**.
Die Deutsche Nationalbibliothek lists this publication in the "Deutsche
Nationalbibliografie"; detailed bibliographic data is available
on the Internet at http://dnb.d-nb.de/.

Cover art: William Faulkner courtesy of Cofield Collection,
Southern Media Archive, University of Mississippi Libraries

The paper in this book meets the guidelines for permanence and durability
of the Committee on Production Guidelines for Book Longevity
of the Council of Library Resources.

© 2011 Peter Lang Publishing, Inc., New York
29 Broadway, 18th floor, New York, NY 10006
www.peterlang.com

All rights reserved.
Reprint or reproduction, even partially, in all forms such as microfilm,
xerography, microfiche, microcard, and offset strictly prohibited.

Printed in Germany

FOR THE TEACHERS WHO HELPED ME
FIND MY VOICE, FROM AUDREY TO NOEL

Contents

Acknowledgments ix
Abbreviations xi

Chapter One
Introduction: "Enlist, or Else" 1

Chapter Two
"Not Like the Usual Pedagogue Lawyer ": Gavin Stevens's Early Appearances and Prototypes 10

Chapter Three
"He Hadn't Expected This": Stevens and Chick Mallison in *Go Down, Moses* and *Intruder in the Dust* 22

Chapter Four
"Justice as He Sees It": *Knight's Gambit* and *Requiem for a Nun* 33

Chapter Five
"The Poet's Romantic Dream": Sir Gawain, Sir Galwyn of Arthgyl, and Stevens in the Snopes Trilogy 56

Chapter Six
"Forming Her Mind": Stevens and Linda Snopes Kohl 78

Chapter Seven
Conclusion: "A Gentleman Can Live Through Anything" 92

Notes 97
Works Cited 109
Index 115

Acknowledgments

I would like to thank the many careful readers who commented on all stages of this manuscript, especially Noel Polk, Maureen Ryan, Ellen Weinauer, Martina Sciolino, Michael Salda, Audrey Watkins, Theresa Towner, Claude Pruitt, Angelia N. Logan, Allison C. Chestnut, Linda McDaniel, Rebecca Jordan, Iris Easterling, and Wyatt Moulds. I am also indebted to Mr. Tommy Covington of the Ripley Public Library, Mr. John Cloy of the University of Mississippi Library, and the staff of the Special Collections Division of Tulane's Howard-Tilton Memorial Library for their invaluable research assistance, as well as to my student research assistants, Breanna Bradley, Elizabeth N. Cluff, and Timothy S. Morris. The administration and English department faculty at William Carey University have provided moral and financial support for my research, without which this book would not be possible. Special thanks go to English Department Chairperson Thomas J. Richardson, Dean of Arts and Letters Myron C. Noonkester, Academic Vice President Garry Breland, and President Tommy King. Thanks also go to Brantley Fryfogle for his valuable technical assistance. Finally, I am grateful for permission to reprint revisions of the following essays:

"Intruder in the Past" © 2006 by the *The Southern Literary Journal* and the University of North Carolina at Chapel Hill Department of English. Reprinted with permission in chapter 3.

"Justice as He Saw It: Gavin Stevens in *Knight's Gambit*." From *The Faulkner Journal*, XIX:2 (Spring 2004). Copyright 2004 by the University of Central Florida. Reprinted with permission in chapter 4.

"William Faulkner's Southern Knights: *Sir Gawain and the Green Knight*, Sir Galwyn of Arthgyl, and Gavin Stevens" © 2006 by the University of Chicago. Reprinted with permission in chapters five and six.

Cover image rights are held by the Cofield Collection, Southern Media Archive, University of Mississippi Libraries.

Abbreviations

The following abbreviations for William Faulkner's texts have been established by *The Faulkner Journal* and appear in parenthetical references:

CS	*Collected Stories of William Faulkner*
ESPL	*Essays, Speeches, and Public Letters*
FD	*Flags in the Dust*
FU	*Faulkner in the University: Class Conferences at the University of Virginia 1957-58*
GDM	*Go Down, Moses*
H	*The Hamlet*
ID	*Intruder in the Dust*
KG	*Knight's Gambit*
LA	*Light in August*
LG	*Lion in the Garden: Interviews with William Faulkner 1926-1962*
M	*The Mansion*
MAY	*Mayday*
R	*The Reivers*
RN	*Requiem for a Nun*
SL	*Selected Letters of William Faulkner*
T	*The Town*
US	*Uncollected Stories of William Faulkner*

• CHAPTER ONE •

Introduction: "Enlist, or Else"

Gavin Stevens . . . was a good man but he didn't succeed in living up to his ideal.

—*William Faulkner* (LG 225)

Near the end of the novella "Knight's Gambit," William Faulkner describes how Gavin Stevens, the Yoknapatawpha county attorney, prevents a crime from occurring by discovering that Max Harriss has purchased Rafe McCallum's unmanageable stallion, a horse "said to have killed two men" (KG 201), and secretly had it delivered to the "little stable" at the Harriss estate (211). Max does so in the hope that the stallion will kill a third man, Captain Gualdres, the "fortune-hunting Spick" that Harriss fears will marry his mother (137). Each night Gualdres trains a nearly blind thoroughbred mare by teaching her to jump in total darkness in order to "teach her the—how you say it?—faith" (217). Max places the stallion in the mare's stable hoping that the horse will attack an unaware Gualdres when he opens the stable door under cover of darkness. His plan almost works; just in time, Stevens discovers that Max has purchased the horse and he warns Gualdres minutes before the captain reaches the stable (212). McCallum, the only man who can control the horse, releases it into the paddock and Gualdres looks on as a "furious mass the color of doom or midnight in a moonward swirling of mane and tail like black flames" comes "screaming" out and rushes McCallum before the man promptly subdues the animal (220).

Meanwhile, Max escapes to Memphis where Stevens has a city police officer pick Max up, tell him that he is "not a prisoner," and ask him to return to Jefferson because Stevens wants "him to come back here and talk" (KG 221). Max does so and points out that, although Stevens may have put an end to his plans for Gualdres, the prosecutor "couldn't prove an intention": "All that you can prove, you wont even have to. I already admit it. I affirm it. I bought a horse and turned it into a private stable on my mother's property" (223). Even so, Stevens gives Max an ultimatum: "Enlist, or else" (224). Max knows that Stevens would have a difficult time proving intent, yet he agrees to enlist after Stevens likens the young man's dealings with Gualdres, his family, and Stevens to a card game:

> Just enlist. Look. You are playing poker (I assume you know poker, or at least—like a lot of people—anyway play it). You draw cards. When you do that, you affirm two things: either that you have something to draw to, or you are willing to support to your last cent the fact that you have not. You dont draw and then throw the cards in because they are not what you wanted, expected, hoped for; not just for the sake of your own soul and pocket-book, but for the sake of the others in the game, who have likewise assumed that unspoken obligation. (225)

Stevens's manipulation of Max attracts my interest for several reasons. By appealing to Max's sense of honor, Stevens convinces him to join the army as punishment for the crime Stevens prevented, despite the fact that World War II looms large and has likely inspired Max's failure to register by the age of twenty-one (KG 224). The analogy Stevens constructs to compel Max to take this drastic action involves poker, a game of chance with which Stevens assumes Max has some familiarity. In convincing Max to act honorably by owning up to his actions and facing a punishment that Stevens thinks befits attempted murder, Stevens essentially calls Max's bluff—or perhaps Max fails to call Stevens's. Stevens persuades Max to punish himself for a crime that did not occur even though (or perhaps more accurately because) as county prosecutor, Stevens has no legal recourse. To extend the analogy of the game, Stevens forces Max to fold, supposedly for his own good, despite the fact that Max holds the winning hand. Either Max is not quite the gambler that Stevens fancies him, or Stevens has stacked the deck against him; either way, Stevens now enjoys a sizeable advantage.

While that exchange involves poker, the game from which the novella falsely appropriates its title, chess, also applies to the situation. In chess, a gambit functions as a tricky opening move in which a player sacrifices a minor piece in order to gain a better position; however, there is no such move as a knight's gambit. Types of gambits that do exist include a Queen's Gambit, a Goring Gambit, and a King's Bishop Gambit, but, as Patrick Samway, S.J., notes, "there does not properly exist a Knight's Gambit, except by analogy" ("Gavin Stevens" 147). In this case Stevens, the knight of the title, sacrifices Max, his unnamed sister, and Captain Gualdres when he has no right to do so. Stevens sends Max off to war and arranges a marriage for his sister to an unwilling Gualdres; the prospective groom even tells Stevens, "In my country, the campo, there is a saying: Married; dead" (KG 227). When Stevens proposes marriage to Melisandre Backus Harriss, his former girlfriend and Max's mother, a scant ten pages later it seems that Stevens may have eliminated the children to avoid facing the same resistance from them that Gualdres met with when courting Melisandre. At the very least, their absence is a welcome benefit of Stevens's manipulations. Faulkner leaves Stevens's motivations ambiguous here, but he makes it quite clear that when the law fails to provide a punishment, Stevens feels he should react. Stevens thinks his own sentence befits Max's crime: Stevens arbitrarily, needlessly, and overzealously punishes Max by sending him into battle, maybe even to his death. Stevens does so not in pursuit of justice, but in pursuit of what Faulkner terms "justice as he sees it" (506), a concept based solely on Stevens's personal judgment.

Faulkner fills his novels with failed idealists pursuing similarly elusive goals, gentlemanly figures like Quentin Compson and Horace Benbow whom scholars have identified with varying sources of inspiration, including Faulkner himself.[1] These idealists are, as Philip Cohen notes, "much given to introspection and tend either to withdraw from life or to engage in quixotic quests." He elaborates:

> Such characters are occasionally used by Faulkner to examine different negative concepts of art and the artist. Faulkner's pity for the plight of such a figure in a world which has no room for him is usually tempered by his awareness that this character is too effete, too lost in the labyrinth of his own consciousness, to live a meaningful existence or to create any lasting art.

These figures "are also usually troubled about women and about sex. Their psyches are torn between acknowledging repressed sexual urges and upholding an idealistic veneration of chaste women" ("Horace Benbow" 78). Faulkner frequently depicts these failed idealists as medieval knights, courtly lovers engaged in dubious quests that involve crusading for the honor of their ladies, seeking justice, and opposing such perceived evils as "Snopesism.

Without question, Gavin Stevens is Faulkner's quintessential idealistic gentleman knight. During a lecture at the University of Virginia, Faulkner even indirectly referred to Stevens as such when he spoke of the "cavalier spirit" that defines these figures: "By cavalier spirit, I mean people who believe in simple honor for the sake of honor, and honesty for the sake of honesty." Although he did not name Stevens specifically, he surely had him in mind and hinted at such a configuration by juxtaposing such figures against the "Snopeses" and their capacity to "cope with the new industrial age" (*FU* 80). Faulkner did not, however, wholeheartedly approve of these gentlemen. As André Bleikasten observes, "Faulkner's sympathy for them never goes without suspicion, and in his fiction there are many hints that idealism is more often than not a mere hiding place from the ugliness of real life" (38).[2] Moreover, Stevens appears more frequently than any other character in Faulkner's fiction, yet he remains one of the most enigmatic.[3] While often "alleged to be the voice of Faulkner," Stevens more accurately functions, as Marion Tangum points out, as a "spokesperson for the good, just, but limited Southern gentleman: limited by upbringing, education, and the history of the South"

(382). David M. Monaghan adds that some scholars identify "a distance between Faulkner and Stevens" that allows the author to adopt "an ironic attitude towards his character" (449). Yet many Faulknerians retain a strong affection for Stevens, at least in part, because he seems so closely connected to Faulkner himself;[4] in fact, Joseph Blotner notes that even Estelle Faulkner "saw in Gavin Stevens quixotic qualities which reminded her of her husband" ("Continuity" 20).

Frequently, Faulkner has Stevens voice opinions quite similar to those that fill his own speeches and public letters, and Stevens similarly stands out like an intellectual sore thumb amongst small town folk who, although they like him, fail to fully understand him. Most scholars no longer think of Stevens as merely Faulkner's mouthpiece, but many still imagine him as the character most resembling Faulkner in all of Jefferson. John T. Irwin writes of Stevens, along with Quentin Compson and Horace Benbow:

> Clearly, Faulkner set out to imagine a twentieth-century male descendent of an aristocratic Southern family, a descendant more or less weighed down by his sense of the past and more or less unsuited by education and temperament for thriving in the modern world, a descendant who personified, if not the South, then the Southern ruling class at a certain point in this century, determined to live in the past by staying enclosed in its own region, self-absorbed with its own image in a way that inevitably reminded Faulkner of the figure of Narcissus. ("Horace Benbow" 543)

Louis D. Rubin, Jr. has argued that Faulkner's juxtaposition of such divergent characters as "Horace Benbow and Bayard Sartoris in *Flags in the Dust*, Quentin Compson and Dalton Ames in *The Sound and the Fury*, Quentin and Thomas Sutpen in *Absalom, Absalom!*, [and] Darl and Jewel Bundren in *As I Lay Dying*" consistently illustrates "not just a division but a dichotomy between the man of sensibility and the man of action" (72). In Stevens, however, Faulkner unifies these two paradoxical figures. Faulkner may depict Stevens as tormented, but he does not paralyze him in the fashion of earlier idealists. Faulkner introduces Stevens into the novels in chapter 19 of *Light in August* (1932) and Stevens supplants Benbow in the fiction from that point forward. Irwin suggests, "the reason that Faulkner needed yet another incarnation of the structure in Gavin Stevens was to explore the possibility that this figure might not end up a youthful suicide or a middle-aged failure but eventually win through to some kind of qualified success in his personal and public life" (544). Even this comes at quite a high cost given the price those surrounding Stevens pay for such "qualified success."

I suspect that Faulkner replaced these early, ineffectual figures with Stevens because his late fiction increasingly required a character more capable of taking action in the plot; accordingly, misreadings of Stevens as the author's mouthpiece, the detached observer, or the stereotypical Southern intellectual stem from the fact that he figures most prominently in Faulkner's fundamentally misunderstood later fiction. Noel Polk notes that readers "have mostly failed to confront the Faulkner of this period in all his complexity" ("Polysyllabic" 299), and Theresa M. Towner adds, "Where the later novels have not suffered direct abuse, they have suffered from neglect that allows early misreadings to stand unchallenged" (*Color Line* 4). These early critical pronouncements conflate Faulkner's public statements of the 1950s with the fiction of that period despite the fact that, as Polk points out, "For all his public testimony to humanity's capacity to renew itself, to endure and prevail, etc., there is no evidence whatsoever to indicate that Faulkner really believed it, and quite a bit of evidence to suggest the opposite" ("Polysyllabic" 314). Morse Peckham proposes that Faulkner wrote speeches such as his optimistic Nobel address for specific occasions that required him to "quite deliberately" resolve "a tension as part of a public appearance," and argues, "It seems reasonable to conclude that Faulkner offered an illusionistic and idealistic sop to the public and that with irony and a certain contempt he played the part of the Noble Idealistic Writer—the kind the Nobel Literary Prize was instituted to reward" (9).

For example, Faulkner's 1955 letter to Else Jonsson concerning his efforts to facilitate racial reform provides a startling example of his hopelessness for humanity during this period:

> I am doing what I can. I can see the possible time when I shall have to leave my native state, something as the Jew had to flee from Germany during Hitler. I hope that wont happen of course. But at times I think that nothing but a disaster, a military defeat even perhaps, will wake America up and enable us to save ourselves, or what is left. This is a depressing letter, I know. But human beings are terrible. One must believe well in man to endure him, wait out his folly and savagery and inhumanity. (*SL* 382)

Polk's assessment does not stand alone. James B. Carothers points to the inherent paradox of the putative schism in the fiction:

> over the last twenty years of his life, Faulkner provided extensive and often invaluable commentary on his art, while during the same period he also produced a body of fiction that his reputation, by most accounts, would be better off without. The current solution to this paradox is usually to employ whatever portion of Faulkner's nonfictional commentary the critic finds useful to supplement the reading of the texts of "the major years," while simultaneously lamenting, regretting, denigrating, ignoring, or otherwise condescending to Faulkner's fiction of the later period. ("Rhetoric" 264)

Towner agrees that the late novels are no less simple "in form and content than their predecessors. . . . Nor are they more optimistic about humanity's fate, or less skeptical of 'human nature'" (*Color Line* 8), and Joseph R. Urgo argues for a similar continuity, suggesting that the Snopes trilogy "represents the assembly of Faulkner's aesthetics into a single, coherent, and wholistic form" (169).

Although these scholars calling for more serious attention to Faulkner's late period remain in the minority even among Faulknerians, the work they have generated shows that Southern and American studies stand to gain much from exploring the focal and stylistic shifts that distinguish the late fiction from Faulkner's earlier work. Joe Craig Wisdom quite logically proposes of this evolution, "as World War I represented the end of many of the old verities which governed human behavior, *A Fable* represents an end of many of the artistic verities which govern Faulkner's work" (3). Wisdom notes that Faulkner replaces one of these "verities," his reliance on a mythic construct of the past, with a consideration of his contemporary world and suggests that readers "search with Faulkner in the novels after *A Fable* not for a mytho-historic truth, but for socio-historic perspective" (4).⁵ Similar lines of inquiry have generated some of the most insightful readings of the late Faulkner to date: Urgo's approach to Faulkner's apocrypha as "a political and ideological alternative to what Faulkner considered to be the totalitarianism of modern society" (*Apocrypha* 4), and his identification of the Snopes trilogy as "apotheosis" of that vision (169); Polk's re-envisioning of *Requiem for a Nun* that regards Temple as a victim instead of a sinner and places her "rather than Nancy . . . at the moral center of the novel" (xiii); and Towner's tracing of the cultural work the late novels perform via the "decidedly new trend in Faulkner's artistry, an evolution in his craftsmanship that reflects his increasing interest in how racial identity is formed and maintained" (*Color Line* 8). While by no means exhaustive, these sufficiently varied examples illustrate issues and concerns in Faulkner's later works which still apply to contemporary American literature and culture. Karl F. Zender proposes that Faulkner's late fiction in general and *Requiem for a Nun* in particular allow "topics formerly only obliquely represented in Faulkner's fiction, female self-affirmation and female bonding across lines of class and race, to emerge into prominence" (*Politics* 132). Zender suggests that this expansion stems from Faulkner's own personal development as he "accepted more of the world—both the world outside himself and the one inside—than any other writer in America" (151).

The growth that Zender describes informed Faulkner's worldview during the late period and provided the impetus for his political activities of the 1950s, ventures into "subjects of global politics and species survival after the war" and the use of his position as "a Southerner with considerable legitimacy in the Northern literary establishment to address the emerging civil rights crisis" (Karaganis 54). In *Children of the Dark House*, Polk offers a compelling analysis of Faulkner's period of political activity when he speculates:

> Faulkner's mid-fifties *engagement*, then, was no simple-minded, knee-jerk response to the mantel of Sage that the Nobel Prize had invested him with, but rather a deeply felt attempt both to repatriate himself into a humanity from which his own giantism and despair had alienated him and to give that same humanity the capacity to face their individual lives without ideological illusion. He wanted, in effect, to give the masses a sign they could understand and respond to, in a language and in a medium they did have access to rather than in the language of his high art. He wanted to persuade them if not to individuality, then at least to their personal *and* collective best interests. (261)

Polk adds that Faulkner abandoned his political interlude after "being beaten over and over by their [the general public's] intractable and inexhaustible commitment to their ideological prisons." In effect, Faulkner realized that even though he "tried his best to engage people on their own terms, using the methods of logical argument and the media they understood, to show them where their ideological commitments were leading everybody, the nation and the world, [...] he failed to change one damned thing" (271).

Faulkner kept trying in his fiction, though. Wisdom notes of the late period:

> the change in Faulkner's writing, as in that of many of the writers during this period, is a direct response to changing global realities. The combination of righteous indignation, mass isolation, and artistic euphoria that resulted in the post-World War I literary outpouring by writers throughout Europe and the Americas was beginning to temper during the 1930s and by the decade that followed had hardened, in general, into a literature of social consciousness born largely of an awareness of the political success and mass appeal of fascism. Faulkner was deeply concerned with the growing power of government and the concomitant loss of individual freedom, especially in the period during and after World War II. (5)

Faulkner's anxieties about the ideology behind such movements perhaps emerges most disturbingly in the form of A *Fable*'s "old general who really believes that he manipulates the belief systems of 'the people' not for personal aggrandizement, either in the pleasure of exercising power or for any type of personal gain, but simply because *they need it*, because they *need* some political or religious credo to provide coherence to their lives" (Polk, "Polysyllabic" 325). Faulkner portrays them as "sheep," eager to be led, and Polk surmises that "in the bleakest reaches of A *Fable*'s themes, there is no alternative to the ideological manipulation of people's minds" (326). Accordingly, Urgo has suggested "that Faulkner is a far more politically challenging and politically radical writer than has yet been explicated in any systematic fashion" and that the "radicalism of his apocrypha has been muted partially because of the personal image he cultivated in the 1950s" (*Apocrypha* 4).

I would suggest that Stevens, the character critics generally consider most similar to Faulkner and (arguably) the most important narrator in the late period, has been equally misunderstood. If we examine Stevens as both a slave to and an agent of the ideology that sustains existing structures of class and power in Yoknapatawpha, he appears to serve a significantly darker purpose than critics have previously recognized. In the following chapters I outline Faulkner's fictional use of and resistance to the figure of the gentleman as a social and historical construct and describe Stevens as Faulkner's definitive gentleman, one who unifies the characteristics of the various Faulknerian permutations. With this basis firmly in place, I juxtapose Stevens's intricate role in the late fiction with his appearances in the early work to illuminate underappreciated social and political aspects of the later fiction. Zender has already described Stevens as "an upholder of an older, prewar tradition of high culture" (*Politics* 140); however, my interest lies in the types of "traditions" he sustains and the methods he uses to do so. Stevens, like *The Fable*'s old general, manipulates others with the best of intentions, but whereas Faulkner's portrait of the helpless masses "seems to justify the old general's paternalism" (Polk, "Polysyllabic" 325), he offers no similar validation for Stevens's actions, and Stevens hides behind a chivalric mask as he takes increasingly destructive measures that affect both himself and others entrusted into his care.

Stevens, then, does not speak for Faulkner or represent the author at a fictional remove as some brand of moral exemplar. Instead, Faulkner uses Stevens as a character deliberately similar to himself to criticize all that he despised in people of his class, and perhaps even some of what he feared might lie within the darkest recesses of his own heart. Stevens, undoubtedly Faulkner's "Good Man," was hardly his "Favorite,"[6] and I suspect that Stevens, with his sliding scale of morality and penchant for pursuing "justice as he sees it" (*RN* 506), terrified Faulkner in ways that few characters could. The complicated role that Stevens's moral code plays in Faulkner's late fiction defies simplistic interpretation and encourages readers to look beyond Stevens's outward façade into the heart of a man who stands as just another example of flawed Faulknerian humanity, one of the "poor frail victims of being alive" that Judith Bryant Wittenberg speaks of (336), or one of the "poor sons of bitches" Reverend Goodyhay prays for in *The Mansion* (584). During one of his interviews in Japan Faulkner said that man's "immortality is that he is faced with a tragedy which he can't beat and he still tries to do something with it" (*LG* 89). Stevens's tragedy is that his ubiquitous idealism blinds him so completely that, when he tries to "do something with it," he usually makes things worse and often never even realizes the extent of the damage he inflicts. As Faulkner said in 1955, Stevens "was a good man but he didn't succeed in living up to his ideal" (*LG* 225). Stevens never realizes his own imperfections, though, and the ideological convictions motivating his actions embody the problem of nobility in Faulkner's late fiction. Regardless of his (mostly) good intentions, Stevens's belief in his own infallibility and his presumption to make the life-altering choices that he deems right and just for others ultimately make him one of Faulkner's most dangerous figures.

The passage from "Knight's Gambit" with which I began this chapter illustrates Stevens's heavy-handed tendencies perfectly. Stevens quite literally wields the old general's power when he sends Max to war, telling him to "Enlist, or else" (224). Max asks Stevens, "What makes you think you or the army or anybody else will ever catch me again?" Stevens, confident in his persuasive abilities, responds, "I hadn't thought about it at all. . . . Would it make you feel better to give me your word?" (225). Max, acting mostly out of his own feelings of guilt, tries to make himself deserving of Stevens's faith in his honor with his willingness to do what Stevens deems best. Max accepts Stevens's judgment and simply stands chastened for a moment with "his head bent a little" before leaving for Memphis to pursue the fate that Stevens has arranged for him (226). The scene spans only a few pages but crystallizes the nature of Stevens's power; others believe Stevens to be a good man, one who knows best, one less confused about life than they are thanks to Harvard, Heidelberg, and his presumptive strong and trustworthy moral compass. Characters trust Stevens because of his self-assured, learned brand of morality, when they should instead fear him for that very reason. The following pages demonstrate that Stevens often engages in similar gambits and in doing so sacrifices many characters—figures that he thinks of as pawns—while pursuing his notions of justice. Ultimately, we might most usefully view Faulkner's depiction of Stevens as the author's own knight's gambit, a tricky opening move that he makes in the later fiction. Faulkner sacrifices Stevens and his moral rhetoric to obtain a more advantageous position, one that allows him to depict the danger inherent in trusting leaders who place themselves above the law in the pursuit of justice as they see it, a concept that, in Stevens's case, all too easily and all too frequently becomes justice as it benefits him. In the end, Faulkner's descriptions of Stevens's manipulations of the law, his misunderstanding of human beings, and his rhetorically high-minded pursuit of "not so much truth as of justice, or of justice as he sees it" (*RN* 505-06) removes Stevens ideologically only a degree or two away from the most terrifying dictators of the 20th century.

• CHAPTER TWO •

"Not Like the Usual Pedagogue Lawyer": Gavin Stevens's Early Appearances and Prototypes

> Quite often the young man will write about himself simply because himself is what he knows best. That he is using himself as the standard of measure, and to simplify things, he writes about himself as—perhaps as he presumes himself to be, maybe he hopes himself to be, or maybe as he hates himself for being. Though after that, the more you write, the more you see you have to write, the more you have learned by writing, and probably don't really have time to identify with a character except at certain moments when the character is in a position to express truthfully things which you yourself believe to be true. Then you'll put your own ideas in his mouth, but they—when you do that they'll become his. I think that you're not trying to preach through the character, that you're too busy writing about people.
>
> —William Faulkner (*FU* 25-26)

Numerous biographers have chronicled William Faulkner's ambiguous relationship with Southern history, but none have done so more fully than Joel Williamson. That connection, as Williamson suggests in *William Faulkner and Southern History*, belongs to the larger pattern of contradiction that characterizes Faulkner's life:

> William Faulkner's writings abound in paradox, and so too does his life. He craved fame and fortune, but he hated the scrutiny that success brought to his personal life. Usually mannerly, sometimes engaging, even warm and easy with children, some relatives, and a few friends, he grew reticent and ultimately surly and insulting when he felt that his own life was under inspection. When forced to emerge into public view against his will, he often stood behind a shield of impeccably correct manners and a reticence that approached taciturnity. At other times, he exhibited a Faulkner manqué, a persona, a Faulkner that was neither appealing nor, objectively considered, very real. (4)

One persona Faulkner cultivated, that of the Southern gentleman, often seemed a transparent mask indeed. When reading Faulkner's comments about his own experience as a Southerner, his claims of spending "five years in the seventh grade" (*LG* 7), of thinking of himself "as a farmer, not a writer" (59), and of learning about psychology not from reading Freud, but from "the characters I have invented and playing poker" (*FU* 268),[1] one would do well to heed Doris Betts's advice to "read with a whole boxful of salt anything southern writers themselves say about the South because they may be truthful, merely polite, bored, or actively fantasizing. Their responses rarely reveal the full context of how they were asked, or by whom" (170). Yet attaining the outward symbols of gentility must have been important to Faulkner given his purchase and renovation of Rowan Oak and subsequent acquisition of Bailey's Woods and Greenfield Farm. In his later years in Virginia, he even joined the Farmington Hunt Club, owned one house in Charlottesville, and was trying to purchase Red Acres, a place "out in the country," when he died (Blotner, *A Biography* [1984] 669).[2]

Faulkner often made conflicted statements about the South in general; however, he did not always speak so ambivalently about his home and the most pressing political issues of his day, particularly about matters of race. As he said in his infamous interview with Russell Howe, "As long as there's a middle road, all right, I'll be on it. But if it came to fighting I'd fight for Mississippi against the United States even if it meant going out into the street and shooting Negroes. After all, I'm not going out to shoot Mississippians" (*LG* 261). When this statement caused a ruckus in the press, Faulkner wrote in a letter to the editor of *The Reporter* that he may have been intoxicated at the time: "They are statements which no sober man would make, nor, it seems to me, any sane man believe" (*LG* 265). He did not exactly deny them, though, as Neil R. McMillen and Noel Polk point out (6), yet Faulkner would later reverse this position completely when he remarked at the University of Virginia, "the only thing that will solve that problem [of racial inequity in 1950s America] is not integration but equality, for the Negro to know that he has just as much and just as valid rights in this country as anybody else has" (*FU* 227). Faulkner gave yet another conflicted response, though; when asked at a press conference upon his arrival at the university about what elements "of the Southern tradition and heritage" he hoped his grandson would inherit, Faulkner replied: "I hope of course that he will cope with his environment as it changes. And, I hope that his mother and father will try to raise him without bigotry as much as can be done. He can have a Confederate battleflag if he wants it, but he shouldn't take it too seriously" (13-14). McMillen and Polk suggest:

> Perhaps the best we can do is admit that Faulkner, for all his genius, was in all kinds of ways as much a citizen of Mississippi as his white neighbors, and necessarily shared,

> in his personal, communal life, many of his community's values. That he managed to transcend these values in his fiction, or at least to demonstrate how problematic they are, does not necessarily mean that he was able to do so in his private life. (13) [3]

After all, they add, "Few people, certainly not William Faulkner, are so uncomplicated as to be of a single mind on the most explosive issues of their time" (13). And as Faulkner said himself: "any man works out of his past, since any man—no man is himself, he's the sum of his past, and in a way, if you can accept the term, of his future too. And this struggle between the South and the North could have been a part of my background, my experience, without me knowing it" (*FU* 47-48).

Faulkner's preoccupation with the ambiguous figure of the Southern gentleman, the product of the Cavalier tradition's influence on the Southern romance, is vital to understanding the parallels and contrasts between Faulkner's fiction and life. The Cavalier myth stems from the notion that a large number of immigrants entering Virginia between 1645 and 1675 were noble supporters of Charles I who fled the repression that followed the victory of Oliver Cromwell's Puritan forces in the English Civil War (R. Watson, "Cavalier" 131).[4] As James C. Cobb explains:

> By the 1830s writers eager to explain why the inhabitants of the northern states and those of the southern states appeared to be so different in values and temperament had begun to seize on the idea that the people of the two regions were simply heirs to the dramatically different class, religious, cultural, and political traditions delineated by the English Civil War. The northern states were populated, so many believed, by the descendants of the middle-class Puritan "Roundheads" who had routed the defenders of the monarchy, the aristocratic Cavaliers, supposedly of Norman descent, who had then settled in the southern states. (22)

Cobb notes that historian David Hackett Fischer "has argued that the 'cavalier thesis' may have some validity for Virginia at least" (22), and adds that although the "allure of the Cavalier ideal for northern readers might seem surprising, especially since the southern planter's aristocratic airs and indulgences had been so repugnant to some earlier northern writers," the "surging egalitarianism of the Jacksonian era seemed to spark a certain 'hankering after aristocracy,' as William R. Taylor put it, among more affluent, better educated Americans in general" (Cobb 24).

This myth underlies the idea of the Old South itself, the chimera of a civilized society governed by gentlemen. As Ritchie D. Watson notes, the "concept of the southern gentleman is inextricably mingled with that of the southern cavalier," and the ideal operates via the "recognition of the inherent inequality of man and the acceptance of the idea that certain men were born to lead and that others, the great majority, were born to follow and serve." Watson continues, "Assured of his own superiority, a gentleman was expected at all times to be graceful and dignified in his deportment, as well as courteous and thoughtful toward all men, regardless of their social status" ("Gentleman" 292). Bertram Wyatt-Brown points out that honor (or at least the idea of it) "came first" in such an order and the "determination of men to have power, prestige, and self-esteem and to immortalize these acquisitions through their progeny was the key to the South's development" (16). The concept of honor "applied to all white classes, though with manifestations appropriate to each ranking. Few could escape it altogether. Gentility, on the other hand, was a more specialized, refined form of honor, in which moral uprightness was coupled with high social position" (88). Wyatt-Brown distills the components "necessary for the public recognition of gentility in the Old South" down to "sociability, learning, and piety" (89);[5] while these categories certainly prove useful, the more telling aspect of his definition involves his focus on the "public recognition" of gentility. Indeed, the actual characteristics a gentleman possessed mattered far less than the public image he projected. Cobb also speaks to the acceptable imperfections of this image:

> the perception of the planter-Cavalier as not quite up to the demands of a rapidly changing contemporary world suggested someone who, however noble, was also flawed, someone whose admirable intentions were often neutralized by ineffectual behavior. The old planters might be gracious hosts and gifted orators, but for all their talk of honor and pride, they were often of little use in a real crisis. (25)

In contrast to Faulkner's men of action, strong leaders modeled after his own grandfather, stand the men of sensibility, most notably the failed idealists Horace Benbow and Gavin Blount, and even the early Gavin Stevens. Faulkner introduces these figures quite early in the fiction, and close examination of their initial appearances points out significant continuities and differences of characterization. In many ways, Stevens seems to literally replace Benbow; Benbow does not reappear in the fiction once Stevens enters, they have similar personalities, and the two men even share common experiences. For example, during World War I, they both work in France with the Y.M.C.A. and take Montgomery Ward Snopes along.[6] In many ways Gavin Blount, the character in Faulkner's Memphis stories usually aligned with Gail Hightower of *Light in August*, seems even more closely linked with Stevens than does Benbow.[7] Some scholars have acknowledged Stevens's and Blount's similar characteristics; for example, Dieter Meindl describes Blount as "the ancestor of Faulkner's folksy and grandiloquent *raconteur* Gavin Stevens" (584) and Robert Woods Sayre describes the "echoes" between the two characters as "very real, yet blurred and distorted, coming from afar" (53). Those "echoes" seem most obvious in Faulkner's 1930 "Rose of Lebanon," a story in which Blount serves as Flag Corporal of the Nonconnah Guards, a "semi-military organization with a skeleton staff of regular army officers and a hierarchate of elective social officers with semi-military designations" (59). Blount holds the highest such office, and his curiosity about Lewis Randolph, a belle at the third ball in 1861 who kissed "a hundred and four men, so that she could give a red rose to Charley Gordon" (60), guides the action as Faulkner weaves her story through Blount's. Randolph and Gordon marry shortly after that ball, and Blount finally gets the opportunity to meet Randolph at a dinner party when she returns to Memphis after a sixty-five year absence.

In addition to sharing an interest in history, Blount and Stevens live under similar conditions. Blount, a thirty-seven-year-old bachelor in "Rose of Lebanon," lives in his father's house with his grandmother and his father's sister while he tends to the few patients left in the medical practice he inherited from his father "as a lawyer inherits his" (59); Stevens, a certified lawyer, similarly lives with his sister Maggie and, according to Chick Mallison, spent his vacations from law school "helping Grandfather be City Attorney" before holding that office himself (*T* 4). Both men also tend to express their views on issues they are ill-equipped to discuss: Blount of the reasons the South failed to win the Civil War ("Rose" 69), and Stevens most notably on the problem of race in *Intruder in the Dust*.[8] Moreover, both men think that they lack the courage to approach the women who intrigue them. Blount suspects "that [he] would never have sent flowers to Lewis Randolph. Could never have. That's a summing, a totality, of breath" (68), and Stevens leaves the door to his office open before his first meeting alone with Eula Varner Snopes in *The Town* because he suspects that he "would probably bolt, flee, run home to Maggie" (79).

To be sure, the two men have much in common, but Faulkner most concretely connects them through their inquisitive natures. Before he has even finished his soup the night of the dinner party, Blount's obsessive curiosity compels him to push Lewis Randolph into revealing the events of her encounter with the five Yankees: she threw boiling milk at one of them and threatened the entire group with a pistol before cursing them with "the strong, prompt, gross obscenity of a steamboat mate." Blount's ploy actually causes Randolph to reenact the moment, and after she throws a bowl filled with soup "at Blount's head" the group's laughter jars her back into reality. Later Ran Gordon tells his mother that Blount "wants to apologise" ("Rose" 71), and he may well wish to do so, but Blount nevertheless accomplishes what he unquestionably set out to achieve, and when he "persuade[s] her [Randolph] at last" to come to dinner (68), he learns the portion of her story that he did not know.[9] Donald Kartiganer describes Blount as "Faulkner's first fictional embodiment of the imaginative memory, his first attempt to characterize the recovery of the past as a form of reenactment: not a commemoration but a reinvention; validating its truth not by pretending to have recorded it *there* but by reproducing it *here*." Kartiganer adds that Blount's "pursuit is not simply reminiscence for its own sake but a process of knowledge, leading him to the single scene he cannot tell: Lewis Randolph's confrontation in her kitchen during the war with five Union soldiers" (53).

Later in *Requiem for a Nun*, Stevens engages in much the same process when he manipulates Temple Drake and convinces her to confess to himself, the governor, and her husband. As Temple puts it:

> I'll have to tell the rest of it in order to tell you why I had to have a dope-fiend whore to talk to, why Temple Drake, the white woman, the all-Mississippi debutante, descendant of long lines of statesmen and soldiers high and proud in the high proud annals of our sovereign state, couldn't find anybody except a nigger dope-fiend whore that could speak her language.... (*RN* 554)

Stevens compels Temple to talk though, as she tells the governor, "We didn't come here at two oclock in the morning to save Nancy Mannigoe. Nancy Mannigoe is not even concerned in this because Nancy Mannigoe's lawyer told me before we ever left Jefferson that you were not going to save Nancy Mannigoe." What they did come for, as Temple says, "is just to give Temple Drake a good fair honest chance to suffer" (562). Of course they also came to satisfy Stevens's curiosity, as Faulkner makes clear when Temple falters and Stevens urges her on with comments such as, "You are drowning in an orgasm of abjectness and moderation when all you need is truth" and "All right. Do you want me to tell it, then?" (*RN* 570, 575).

Even as Faulkner develops Benbow and Blount, Stevens first appears as a separate character in the short stories "Smoke," which Faulkner wrote in 1930 and *Harper's Bazaar* published in 1932 (Blotner, *A Biography* [1984] 255, 297), and "Hair," which *American Mercury* published before "Smoke" but the sending schedule suggests that Faulkner most likely composed after "Smoke" (Dunlap 8, Meriwether 172-75). In Stevens's early fictional appearances, we see the beginnings of traits and habits that will define him in Faulkner's later works. The narrator of "Hair" first describes Stevens as "the district attorney, a smart man: not like the usual pedagogue lawyer and office holder" (CS 144). This narrator, as Mary Montgomery Dunlap points out, sounds suspiciously like V.K. Ratliff (12), and he shows that the Stevens of "Hair," like the fully developed character, tends to observe and meddle in the affairs of others. In fact the narrator reveals that after he "met Stevens on a Memphis train," Stevens "suggested I try the road [as a salesman] and got me my position with this company" (CS 144). "Hair" foreshadows elements of the Stevens / Ratliff relationship in the Snopes trilogy, especially in its focus on the narrator's and Stevens's observations of Hawkshaw, a barber whose secret the narrator discovers accidentally and "never [tells] anybody except Gavin Stevens" (144). The narrator learns of Hawkshaw's determination to fulfill the dying wish of his fiancée, Sophie Starnes, by caring for her family after her death and even paying off the mortgage on the family home in Division, a small town "on the State line between Mississippi and Alabama" (137).

The story ends when Stevens takes readers outside the narrator's limited perspective by revealing the final bit of information to solve the mystery that is Hawkshaw. After the narrator returns from a combined business trip and fact-finding expedition to Division, Stevens hints that something significant has occurred during his absence when he asks, "You haven't heard?" (CS 145) and then prompts the narrator to reveal what he has discovered in Division. The narrator complies and Stevens responds, "I didn't think you had heard" (147). Stevens then tells him that after Hawkshaw made the final mortgage payment, he returned to Jefferson to marry Susan Reed, a girl resembling Sophie in whom Hawkshaw has shown interest since he gave her her first haircut. The information comes as a surprise because the narrator has assumed Hawkshaw lost interest in Susan because of her reportedly promiscuous behavior; as the narrator puts it, "the girl went bad on him" (147). Dunlap points out that in the conclusion Stevens "possesses the calm interest and the unperturbed attention belonging to Ratliff of *The Town*" (13),[10] but the final pages also show that Stevens's desire to be in the know and to reveal that knowledge to a limited audience in grand dramatic fashion remains unchanged. As Jay Watson puts it, "the coyness with which he [Stevens] plays his final card is an index of how much he enjoys the contest in which he has been engaged" (81).

In addition to this curiosity about the affairs of others, in the final section of "Hair" Stevens evidences another trait that will later become typical when he basically ignores the narrator's interjections as he, Stevens, tells his portion of the story; the narrator even notices and thinks to himself, "Stevens went on like he wasn't listening to me much" (147). Moreover, the story's narrative focus silences its major female character, Susan Reed, much as Faulkner will silence female characters in later works, most notably Temple Drake Stevens and Eula Varner Snopes. As Theresa M. Towner and James B. Carothers point out, "when we consider that he [Hawkshaw] is forty-five and she [Susan Reed] seventeen or eighteen, and when we notice that we are never privy to Susan's thoughts and experiences, including how she feels about Hawkshaw, the happily-ever-after glow of the story's ending dims a bit" (75).

Faulkner reveals much more about Stevens's features and history when he again appears briefly in *Light in August* in 1932:

> He is the District Attorney, a Harvard graduate, a Phi Beta Kappa: a tall, loosejointed man with a constant cob pipe, with an untidy mop of irongray hair, wearing always loose and unpressed dark gray clothes. His family is old in Jefferson; his ancestors owned slaves there and his grandfather knew (and also hated, and publicly congratulated Colonel Sartoris when they died) Miss Burden's grandfather and brother. He has an easy quiet way with country people, with the voters and the juries;

he can be seen now and then squatting among the overalls on the porches of country stores for a whole summer afternoon, talking to them in their own idiom about nothing at all. (727)

He plays a minor role in the novel, seeing off Joe Christmas's grandparents, the Hineses, at the train station and voicing his theory about Christmas's motivations for murdering Joanna Burden. The details of this short section, however, look ahead to roles and attitudes that will later come to define Stevens. We learn that Stevens takes an active interest in and responsibility for those he thinks of as incapable when he promises the Hineses that he will "see that the boy [Joe Christmas] is on the train in the morning" after his execution (728), much as he will later promise Miss Worsham to bring home Butch Beauchamp's body in *Go Down, Moses* (275). For all his good intentions, Stevens makes outrageous assumptions about others when he speculates of Mrs. Hines that "all she wanted was that he [Christmas] die 'decent', as she put it. Decently hung by a Force, a principle" (*LA* 728). Later he similarly thinks of Mollie Beauchamp's feelings about Butch: "*It doesn't matter to her now. Since it had to be and she couldn't stop it, and now that it's over and done and finished, she doesn't care how he died. She just wanted him home, but she wanted him to come home right*" (*GDM* 281).

Stevens's elaborate explanation of the war between Christmas's "black" and "white" blood, the "successions of thirty years before that which had put that stain either on his white blood or his black blood, whichever you will, and which killed him" is easily the most damning early example of his tendency to jump to far-fetched conclusions:

> But his blood would not be quiet, let him save it. It would not be either one or the other and let his body save itself. Because the black blood drove him first to the negro cabin. And then the white blood drove him out of there, as it was the black blood which snatched up the pistol and the white blood which would not let him fire it. And it was the white blood which sent him to the minister, which rising in him for the last and final time, sent him against all reason and all reality, into the embrace of a chimaera, a blind faith in something read in a printed Book. Then I believe that the white blood deserted him for the moment. Just a second, a flicker, allowing the black to rise in its final moment and make him turn upon that on which he had postulated his hope of salvation. It was the black blood which swept him by his own desire beyond the aid of any man, swept him up into that ecstasy out of a black jungle where life has already ceased before the heart stops and death is desire and fulfillment. And then the black blood failed him again, as it must have in crises all his life. (*LA* 731)

Stevens's ridiculous conjecture tells readers much more about his own attitudes than it does about what actually happened, especially given that Faulkner makes Christmas's racial identity deliberately indeterminate. Moreover, Stephen E. Meats quite logically deduces that Christmas might not even have committed the murder, that "any person, the sheriff or the reader, judging from the evidence we are given *in the novel*, should conclude that Joe Christmas' guilt is an assumption and nothing more" (277).[11] Jay Watson perhaps puts it best when he says that Stevens's "speculations about the last desperate moments of Joe Christmas are at best shaky, at worst racist and absurd" (93).

Finally, other characters in Faulkner's early depictions of Stevens also possess characteristics that Stevens will later take on. The narrator of "Hair," for instance, describes Hawkshaw as "a bachelor born" and a man "born single and forty years old" who, like Stevens, marries late (137). The narrator also says that Hawkshaw "wont be the first man to tilt at windmills" (144); he certainly is not the last. Stevens frequently engages in similarly useless endeavors; indeed, at the University of Virginia, Faulkner asserted that Stevens "seemed a little bit like Don Quixote" in that he presented "a constant sad and funny picture" of a "knight that goes out to defend somebody who don't want to be defended" (*FU* 141). Most notably, though, Hawkshaw's cultivation of a relationship with the much younger Susan Reed resembles Stevens's pursuit of Linda Snopes. When another barber, Maxey, asks Hawkshaw why he "had worked for a year each in six or eight different towns in Alabama and Tennessee and Mississippi," Hawkshaw replies, "I was just looking around" (142). Apparently he "was just looking around" for a replacement for Sophie, much as Stevens transfers a portion of his devotion for Eula to Linda by spending time with her and "forming her mind" even before her mother's death (*T* 158); once Hawkshaw sees Susan Reed, he stays put save for "those two-weeks' vacations of his in April" when he travels to Division to tend to the Starnes house and pay the mortgage (135). The narrator of "Hair" also sounds much like Ratliff evaluating Stevens when he remarks of Hawkshaw, "It beats the devil how the folks that love a woman will let her fool them" (135),[12] and Susan resembles Linda in key ways. For example, both children come from indistinct origins: Susan "was an orphan" and some believed that she "was a niece or a cousin or something" to the Burchett family who took her in (131). Stevens often refers to Flem as Linda's "*so-called father*" (*M* 711), and while readers know that Linda's biological father is Hoake McCarron, as far as we know she does not learn that fact until *The Mansion* (489). Hawkshaw also watches Susan "pass the barber shop each morning and afternoon" ("Hair" 132) just as Stevens watches from his office while planning a "carefully timed accident" that will bring him into contact with Linda. Stevens has obviously watched for her before because he knows the route that she takes each morning. When she fails to pass by the office, he knows that he "had missed her somehow: either taken my post not soon enough or she had taken another route to school" (*T* 179). Finally, both girls matured early, albeit in different ways. The narrator notes that Susan "got grown fast. Too fast. That was the trouble" ("Hair" 133). He reveals the sexual nature of this "trouble" by elaborating, "It's not that she was bad. There's not any such thing as a woman born bad, because they are all born bad, born with the badness in them. The thing is, to get them married before that badness comes to a natural head" (133). After sending Linda to Greenwich Village instead of college Stevens similarly says of her, "Too much has happened to her since [her mother's death]. Too much, too fast, too quick. She outgrew colleges in about twenty-four hours two weeks ago" (307), and she indeed returns to Jefferson a changed woman.

In slightly different fashion, Faulkner goes on to displace and develop traits that Stevens already possesses in "The Tall Men," a story featuring the McCallum family as poor hill whites. The marshal, Mr. Gombault, tries to convince a draft board representative, Mr. Pearson, that the McCallums are not "*people who lie about and conceal the ownership of land and property in order to hold relief jobs which they have no intention of performing, standing on their constitutional rights against having to work*" (CS 46). Gombault demonstrates that the family has little use for government assistance; they even refuse to accept a government subsidy for raising less cotton "when the Government first begun to interfere with how a man farmed his own land." As they tell the county agent who tries to explain the program to them, "we're much obliged. . . . But we don't need no help" (55-56). They turn to raising "whiteface cattle" instead and even go to "the agricultural college to learn right about" how to raise them (57). Ultimately Gombault shows that the boys Pearson criticizes for refusing to do the one thing the government asks "*of them in return* [for assistance programs], *one thing simply, which is to put their names down on a selective-service list*" (46), do so due to a misunderstanding similar to the one concerning the cotton subsidy. Faulkner makes this clear when Pearson arrives at the McCallum home and Gombault tells Rafe McCallum, "He's got a warrant for the boys." Rafe questions, "You mean we have declared war?" (47). Both Buddy and "Old Anse" McCallum fought for their countries, but they enlisted willingly after a declaration of war: Anse volunteered to fight in the Civil War, and since his "ma was a Carter . . . wouldn't nothing do him but to go all the way back to Virginia to do his fighting" (54). Buddy "come along late, late enough to be in the other war, in France in it" and even "bought back two medals, an American medal and a French one, and no man knows till yet how he got them, just what he done" (55). It's not that the family is unwilling to serve the government they refuse to take assistance from; they simply do not understand the "new law" about the "draft business" (50). When Pearson shows up, Anse and Lucius think they have been called into service and willingly prepare to leave.

Towner and Carothers point out that the "story's patriotic themes come in for praise and blame by turns" and that its "tone has been roundly condemned as 'didactic'" (30-31); they add that critical opinion of "The Tall Men" varies widely and note that Faulkner wrote the story primarily from specific financial motivations (29-31).¹³ "The Tall Men" is of interest here, though, because it mentions Stevens in passing as the lawyer Buddy McCallum consults not "for legal advice about how to sue the Government or somebody into buying the cotton, even if they never had no card for it, but just to find out why" (56-57). Apparently the McCallums trust Stevens, and he seems to convey that the cotton incentive is not the charity they fear it may be; after hearing Stevens's explanation, Buddy McCallum says, "I was for going ahead and signing up for it" if "that's going to be the new rule." However, the family decides against it after they "talked it over" because Jackson, the eldest brother "said father would have said no" (57).

Here Stevens appears wholly admirable, at least in Buddy's estimation, but Faulkner assigns to Pearson some of the less attractive qualities that Stevens has already exhibited in another story. James Ferguson describes the investigator as "a necessary but somewhat obvious narrative *device* for the development of the platitudinous thematic material of the story" who "remains on the periphery" of the action (100), but Faulkner also uses Pearson to develop traits he earlier assigned to Stevens in a very similar situation. Pearson "had been in relief work in the state several years, dealing almost exclusively with country people, so he still believed he knew them" (48). Although Pearson thinks he "knows" the McCallums, or at least people of their ilk, when confronted with a room "so filled with tremendous men cast in the same mold as the man who had met them that the very walls themselves must bulge," he "looked about him not only with amazement but with something very like terror" (CS 49). About a year earlier, Faulkner had written a similar scene in "Go Down, Moses" that he would later use in the novel of that same name.¹⁴ Therein Stevens presumes to understand Mollie Beauchamp's feelings about her son's death,¹⁵ yet when he visits the room in which she mourns her son, he grows increasingly uncomfortable and finally "descended the stairs, almost running. It was not far now; now he could smell it, feel it—the breathless and simple dark, and now he could manner himself to pause and wait, turning at the door, watching Miss Worsham as she approached" (264-65). Stevens admits that he should not have come and asks Miss Worsham's forgiveness. Stevens is right; he should not have come because he does not seem to learn anything. He leaves Miss Worsham's house and the next day assumes that Mollie "doesn't care how he [Butch Beauchamp] died" (266).

After (perhaps) coming to appreciate the McCallums as real people rather than as abstract types, Pearson helps the marshal to bury the leg that Doctor Schofield amputated after Buddy McCallum slipped and caught it "in the hammer mill" (CS 47). The marshal's remark to Pearson, "I reckon we can go back to town now" (61), implies that Pearson will find a way to void the warrant for Anse and Lucius because he has comprehended what the marshal wanted him to learn:

> Life has done got cheap, and life ain't cheap. Life's a pretty durn valuable thing. I don't mean just getting along from one WPA relief check to the next one, but honor and pride and discipline that make a man worth preserving, make him of any value. That's what we got to learn again. Maybe it takes trouble, bad trouble, to teach it back to us. . . . (60)

It would seem that Faulkner allows Pearson practical knowledge of and insight into the character of man that Stevens can experience only abstractly, or perhaps will allow himself to experience only in the abstract. However, as John T. Matthews points out, Faulkner does not resolve the situation so neatly:

> As . . . Gombault mounts his windy paean to yeomanry, we may be tempted to overlook the small ways Faulkner deflates his pronouncement. The draft investigator, whose suspicion of "country people" stands to be won, remains inattentive to the story he's told, and ends up assisting in a partial funeral, the comedy of which nearly punctures the tale. Faulkner all but gives away his joke, Buddy's disfiguration by cliché—hasn't got a leg to stand on; one foot in the grave—as if the author has a hard time taking this seriously himself. In such snags Faulkner may signal a kind of critical resistance to his own production of Southern exoticism and patriotic war stock for the magazines. ("Faulkner's Stories" 228)

The chapters that follow this one examine Faulkner's use of similar "snags" to encourage readers to question the purity of Stevens's motivations and the wisdom, or lack thereof, behind many of his decisions and actions. While such observations and connections make for interesting enough markers for the evolution of Stevens as a character, they also document the time and care that Faulkner devoted to that process. Faulkner assigned Stevens some traits that remained constant from the beginning, but he discarded others. Faulkner developed traits in the characters surrounding Stevens that he would later reassign to him, and he even used other characters to develop traits that Stevens had displayed earlier. Faulkner began writing about Stevens in the early 1930s and continued to do so into the 1950s. After the fashion this chapter's epigraph suggests, Faulkner places some of his own beliefs into the mouth of perhaps the single most significant narrator in his late fiction. The following chapters will show, however, that those ideas then become Stevens's alone. As Faulkner said at West Point, "I think that any book should have on the first page, 'The author declines to accept responsibility for the behavior or actions or speeches of any of these characters, because he is simply trying to tell you a story'" (*West Point* 118).

• CHAPTER THREE •

"He Hadn't Expected This": Stevens and Chick Mallison in *Go Down, Moses* and *Intruder in the Dust*

> We're not concerned with death. That's nothing: any handful of petty facts and sworn documents can cope with that. That's all finished now; we can forget it. What we are trying to deal with now is injustice. Only truth can cope with that. Or love.
>
> —Gavin Stevens (*RN* 532)

Gavin Stevens perhaps never speaks truer words, even if he does so inadvertently, than the ones he utters to Temple Drake Stevens in Act I of *Requiem for a Nun* after a jury has already tried, convicted, and sentenced Nancy Mannigoe to death for the crime of murdering Temple's daughter: "What we are trying to deal with now is injustice. Only truth can cope with that. Or love" (*RN* 532). Though the "injustice" and "truth" Stevens speaks of have more to do with Temple's past than with Nancy's fate (and Temple's immediate concern), Stevens is right in saying that only truth and love can cope with injustice, a point Faulkner demonstrates in both *Go Down, Moses* and *Intruder in the Dust*. Stevens hardly represents the power of these concepts himself in these narratives; rather his nephew, Chick Mallison, embodies the strength of love, truth, and, moreover, faith.

Stevens enters *Go Down, Moses* late in the novel's action, much as he does in *Light in August*, and seems, at best, as confused in this novel as in the other. Most notably, Stevens cannot face, much less comprehend, Mollie Worsham Beauchamp's stark display of grief in the final pages. While his "desperate sense of suffocation and nausea" does suggest, as Richard C. Moreland points out, the depth of Stevens's "unacknowledged sense of involvement" in the situation (*Faulkner's Modernism* 292), he nevertheless runs from Mollie, escapes "down the hall fast, almost running; he did not even know whether she was following him or not. *Soon I will be outside*, he thought. *Then there will be air*, *space, breath*" (GDM 278). At worst, Stevens risks coming off as an arrogant bigot when he assumes of Mollie's feeling about her grandson's death:

> It doesn't matter to her now. Since it had to be and she couldn't stop it, and now it's all over and done and finished, she doesn't care how he died. She just wanted him home, but she wanted him to come home right. She wanted that casket and those flowers and the hearse and she wanted to ride through town behind it in a car. (281)

Jay Watson notes that the meaning of this statement depends on what Stevens "means by the word 'right.' If he means 'fairly' or 'justly,' the interpretation seems in accordance with the dignity Mollie has commanded throughout the story, but if he means merely 'proper' or 'correct,' he risks another racist misreading" (105-06). Watson surmises, "It is hard to decide which opinion Stevens entertains, and on this ironic, mystifying note, he returns to his desk and the story concludes. From solving enigmas, the county attorney has gone on to become one" (106). Regardless of the sense in which Stevens uses the word "right," he makes some astonishing assumptions in this passage, ones that make his opinion quite clear; for example, how can he know that Mollie does not "care" how her grandson died? How can he know that she wants to ride behind the hearse? He cannot, and, moreover, he does not even try to understand. He simply retreats to more familiar territory yet again by insisting, "Let's get back to town. I haven't seen my desk in two days" (281).

Stevens's unwillingness (or inability) to understand Mollie foreshadows his assumption of Lucas Beauchamp's guilt in *Intruder in the Dust*, the first novel in which Stevens assumes a major role as a pseudo-father figure and moral guide to his nephew, Chick. Faulkner began writing *Intruder in the Dust* in January of 1948, but he mentioned the project as a potential short story as early as June of 1940 when he described it to Robert K. Haas at Random House as "a mystery story, original in that the solver is a negro, himself in jail for the murder," who "solves the murder in self defense" (SL 128). Although Faulkner expanded his idea into a novel-length manuscript, it essentially follows this original premise, but the jailed man, Lucas Beauchamp, does not solve the mystery alone. After the sheriff, Hope Hampton, arrests Lucas for allegedly shooting Vinson Gowrie, Lucas spies Chick in the crowd as Hampton leads him toward the jail. Lucas says to Chick, "Tell your uncle I wants to see him" (317), and Chick obliges by arranging a meeting between Stevens and Lucas. However, Lucas rightly doubts that lawyer Stevens can help him and actually seeks Chick's assistance. As he tells Chick, "Young folks and womens, they aint cluttered. They can listen. But a middle-year man like your paw and your uncle, they cant listen. They aint got time. They're too busy with facks" (337). Lucas then convinces Chick to violate Gowrie's grave and help him obtain the evidence that he knows will establish his innocence, proof that Gowrie was shot by someone else's gun.

This plot features the relationship between Stevens and Chick, a bond that remains strong throughout the fiction. Indeed, Patrick Samway, S.J., describes it as "One of the strongest familial relationships that exists in Yoknapatawpha," even though it "is not, as one might imagine from an *a priori* point of view, between Chick Mallison and his mother, nor even between Chick and his father." This particularly unique uncle-nephew relationship, Samway notes, "never remained static but evolved constantly as the two characters involved grew older and matured" ("Gavin Stevens" 144). This relationship also seems remarkably reciprocal in that while Chick does glean the best from his Uncle Gavin's lessons, Chick also teaches Stevens much about how to interact with others different from him. As Jay Watson puts it, "uncle and nephew also enjoy moments of genuine intellectual communion, exciting moments in which Chick partakes of Gavin's deep learning in the lore of Yoknapatawpha and in which, later on, Stevens appreciatively learns from his erstwhile student" (112).

The most crucial of such lessons resides in the pages, and in the title, of *Intruder in the Dust*, the novel that foregrounds Chick as one of Stevens's most adept protégés, one who learns far more than Stevens is capable of teaching him. The question of whom readers should envision as the intruder of that title seems almost as complex as the mystery contained within the pages of the novel itself. The lack of any definite candidate, combined with Faulkner's difficulty in selecting a title, tempts one to treat his choice as a throwaway, unimportant because chosen in a moment of desperation. The beginnings of such frustration certainly appear in a letter Robert K. Haas received from Faulkner on March 15, 1948, in which he complained, "By the way, first time in my experience, I cant find a title." Actually, he already knew that he wanted to use the phrase "in the dust," and searched only for the perfect word to combine with it. He wrote to Haas, "I want a word, a dignified (or more dignified) synonym for 'shenanigan,' 'skulduggery'; maybe" (SL 264-65). Faulkner's correspondence shows that his mild irritation at his inability to choose a title soon escalated, and he followed his first letter with another to Haas approximately a week later proposing *Intruder in the Dust* as a title, along with several other possible (though perhaps not completely serious) combinations including the likes of "IMPOSTER," "SLEEPER," "MALFEASANCE," and even "MALAPROP" (265). After initially composing the letter, Faulkner returned to it six hours later and typed, "I believe INTRUDER IN THE DUST is best yet," and even added in ink on the following Tuesday, "Still like INTRUDER IN THE DUST" (265). Clearly, the matter continued to prey upon his mind, and he did not settle it so easily. On April 20, Faulkner, still in search of a title, again wrote to Haas that he sought a word synonymous with "substitution by sharp practice." Although "JUGGLERY" came closest to expressing the meaning he searched for, he rejected it because he thought it a "harsh ugly word" (266). He finally settled firmly upon the title, though not without reservations, by the time he wrote to Bennett Cerf in early May: "lacking any short word for substitution, swap, exchange, sleight-of-hand, I think INTRUDER IN THE DUST is best" (268).

Faulkner's emphasis on the process of substitution puts forward two characters as possible intruders: Jake Montgomery, the "shoestring" timber buyer whose dead body Chick Mallison, Miss Habersham, and Aleck Sander find literally intruding upon the ground of Vinson Gowrie's grave, and Lucas Beauchamp, the black man who stands accused of Gowrie's murder after essentially intruding into the scam which led to that death. The meaning of the title perhaps should depend more upon the phrase "in the dust" than upon the initial, elusive word that Faulkner never quite found adequate. From the beginning, he seemed sure of the final part of his title, and Samway implies that the latter phrase might occupy a more central position than the word that precedes it. As Samway notes in his introduction to the novel's concordance, Faulkner uses the word "intruder" only in the title, but that the phrase "in the dust" is "used 3 times and in each case there is an association with blacks" (ix). Samway's observation, though astute, limits the importance of the central image (dust) by focusing on the entire phrase. Reducing this phrase to its essential image expands the implications of the title. Various forms of "dust" float throughout the pages of *Intruder in the Dust*; an examination of that dust in its various guises gives clues to the intruder's identity and, perhaps more importantly, clarifies Chick's role and the nature of the intrusion.

Faulkner refers to many types of soil in *Intruder in the Dust*, and they all serve specific functions. His deliberate usage emphasizes the importance of such subtle differences; for example, as Chick and Stevens drive through the streets of Jefferson after Chick's all-night adventure in the graveyard, Chick notices the "string of cars and trucks stained with country mud and dust" (385). Faulkner carefully differentiates "mud" from "dust," and such specificity undercuts the otherwise likely possibility that the dust of his title simply refers to the dust of Vinson Gowrie's or, for that matter, any other, grave. But Faulkner never associates any of the novel's various graves with the word "dust": Aleck Sander and Chick shovel "dirt" from Vinson Gowrie's grave (360-61), "dirt" trickles back into it after Hope Hampton later finds it empty (409), Jake Montgomery's body resides in a "mound of fresh shaled earth" (415), and the Gowrie family pulls Vinson's body from "quicksand" (416).

Whatever elements compose the dust in this novel, they seem to come from a source other than the cemetery. Faulkner's most intriguing reference to dust suggests a connection with a passing of another sort and has more to do with Jefferson's mythic history than with any one specific person. As Chick first enters the jail with Stevens, whose legal services Lucas wishes to retain, he remembers:

his uncle had said once that not courthouses nor even churches but jails were the true records of a county's, a community's history, since not only the cryptic forgotten initials and words and even phrases cries of defiance and indictment scratched into the walls but the very bricks and stones themselves held, not in solution but in suspension, intact and biding and potent and indestructible, the agonies and shames and griefs with which hearts long since unmarked and unremembered *dust* had strained and perhaps burst. (emphasis added, *ID* 320-21)

For Chick and, of course, for Stevens, the jail evokes the very essence of Jefferson's strife-filled past. As the various individuals become absorbed into this shared communal history, the "dust," all that remains of the particular hearts, stays, for the most part "unmarked and unremembered" in that collective past. Thus Faulkner's complex construction loosely equates "dust" with some sort of past communal strife and employs the jail as a symbol of it. Accordingly, Faulkner's language reinforces this connection in that the jail gives off a decidedly "dusty" aura as the "dim dusty flyspecked bulb" which lights the jail generates, at best, a "dusty glare" (325-26). Lucas, while held in the very heart of that dusty jail, the lone cell, convinces Chick to obtain the evidence that will prove his innocence. In doing so, Chick unearths something far more disturbing than a dead body; he discovers the depth of Jefferson's ingrained racial prejudices and recognizes the lengths to which its citizens will go to maintain their self-serving ideology of white supremacy.

This realization, though, happens gradually, and Chick's relationship to the history represented by the jail is complicated. The building occupies such a representative position, Chick theorizes, "because it and one of the churches were the oldest buildings in the town, the courthouse and everything else on or in the Square having been burned to rubble by Federal occupation forces after a battle in 1864. More importantly, Chick goes on to establish that the jail stands as such a monument because "scratched into one of the panes of the fanlight beside the door was a young girl's single name, written by her own hand into the glass with a diamond in that same year" (*ID* 321). Though he does not refer to her by name, Chick most likely speaks of the town legend concerning Cecilia Farmer that Faulkner later recounts more fully in *Requiem for a Nun*. Though the various characters seem a bit fuzzy about the details, apparently Cecilia, the jailer's daughter, fell in love at first sight with an army lieutenant whom she spied from the window of the jail. To mark the moment, she scratched her name and the date, "*April 16th 1861*" (*RN* 627), into the glass of the window with her grandmother's ring and watched through that pane for several years, anticipating the lieutenant's return. When he does indeed come back to Jefferson, he and Cecilia supposedly marry, leave Mississippi for a farm in Alabama, and go on to raise a family that includes a dozen sons (627-49). Theresa Towner describes Cecilia's inscription as "a gesture that speaks to someone else's imagination" (*Introduction* 66). Chick certainly feels something akin to such an identification and perhaps imagines that, like the stranger in *Requiem for a Nun*, he can detect in Cecilia's signature a message "from the long long time ago: '*Listen, stranger; this was myself: this was I*'" (*RN* 649). In order to maintain this connection, Chick visits the jail to look through that pane of glass "two or three times a year" and "realise again the eternality, the deathlessness and changelessness of youth" (*ID* 321).

Cecilia's story, then, for Chick both represents the sort of conflict that his uncle's complicated reference concerning dust highlights and gives him a context for his own musings about the past and how history might remember him in a similar fashion. Appropriately enough, this Civil War story grounds that strife at the crux of the South's racially troubled past, and Chick's identification with Cecilia intensifies as the novel progresses. Chick admits that with his efforts on Lucas's behalf, he wants "to leave his mark too on his time in man but only that, no more than that, some mark on his part in earth" (*ID* 430). In attempting to leave this mark, though, Chick, perhaps like Cecilia with her twelve sons, gets far more than he bargained for:

> certainly he hadn't expected this:—not a life saved from death nor even a death saved from shame and indignity nor even the suspension of a sentence but merely the grudging pretermission of a date; not indignity shamed with its own shameful cancellation, not sublimation and humility with humility and pride remembered nor the pride of courage and passion nor of pity nor the pride and austerity and grief, but austerity itself debased by what it had gained, courage and passion befouled by what they had had to cope with.... (430)

Indeed, self-interest motivates Chick when he agrees to help Lucas; he initially wants only to eradicate the childhood debt that he incurs as the novel begins, and he secretly hopes that he might become a significant part of Jefferson's history in the process. Although he only wants to leave his mark on that collective history, as he thinks Cecilia did, he instead comes to see the crowd that almost lynches Lucas, "his people his blood his own," as "a Face monstrous unravening omniverous and not even uninsatiate" (430). In the process of helping Lucas, Chick inadvertently destroys his world as he knows it by putting the events into motion that sever the philosophical and emotional ties binding him to it. Thus he intrudes into this conflict at what, for him, becomes quite a high price.

As Chick watches the mob gather and recognizes that, to the white citizens of Jefferson, Lucas remains largely incidental to his own impending trial for murder, Faulkner writes, "something like a skim or a veil like that which crosses a chicken's eye and which he [Chick] had not even known was there went flick! from his own [eye] and he saw them [the townspeople] for the first time." Chick realizes that the townspeople have "already condemned" Lucas, and only wait "to see that Beat Four should not fail its white man's high estate" (*ID* 387). Chick gradually begins to adjust to his changed vision in the pages that follow. As he rides with his uncle to the exhumation, the car slows and Chick surveys, with a palpable sense of forlorn nostalgia, "his whole native land, his home—the dirt, the earth which had bred his bones and those of his fathers for six generations" as a panoramic map "unfolding beneath him" (398). On the next page, Faulkner writes of Chick and those who people this vista, the ones among whom Chick has lived his entire life: "soon there would not even be any contact since the very mutual words they used would no longer have the same significance and soon after that even this would be gone because they would be too far asunder even to hear one another" (399).

In keeping with his alignment of dust with Jefferson's racially troubled past, Faulkner employs a related image to illustrate Chick's painful adjustment to his dawning cognizance of it. As he returns to Jefferson after discovering Vinson Gowrie's empty grave, Chick first notices "something hot and gritty inside his eyelids like a dust of ground glass." This seems a unique sort of dust, however, because "no simple dust refused as this did to moisten at all with blinking" (*ID* 420). While this "dust" could simply result from Chick's sleepless night, it nevertheless reflects his emotional state as well because Faulkner continues to refer to it at key narrative moments. We see Chick again "blinking painfully his painful moistureless eyelids" as he watches the Square empty from what almost became Lucas's lynching (423). And, finally, Chick describes "the dry hot gritty feel of his skull" as he watches the composite "face" of the mob leaving the Square become "one back of one Head one fragile mushfilled bulb indefensible as an egg yet terrible in its concorded unanimity rushing not at him but away" (428). As Faulkner opens Chick's eyes, he also fills them with the metaphoric dust of the past, and Chick does not easily adjust to all that he can now see.

In the context of his emerging awareness, Chick has to struggle not only with feelings about his own past actions but also with his uncle's theories about matters of race and society. As usual, Stevens talks a good game when he repeatedly refers to the South's duty to resolve the racial problems of its own making, but Erik Dussere points out:

> Gavin's views are given a great deal of authority and textual space, and ultimately he triumphs over Charles's objections to his assertion that the South must repay its own debts–but the book also suggests that Gavin is not to be trusted completely. This is surprising, given that Gavin's endless speeches seem to form the polemical core of the book, and that, Charles tells us, Gavin "had for everything an explanation not in facts but long since beyond dry statistics into something far more moving because it was truth" (49). But the book's failure to endorse Gavin's views on race makes sense in the context of Faulkner's other books. Throughout his career in Faulkner's fiction (with the possible exception of *Requiem for a Nun*), Gavin appears as the very image of the obtuse liberal: certain that he knows what is best for Southern blacks, his pronouncements are forever undercut by the actions of black characters in the text. (52)

Dunlap also notes of the disconnect between Stevens's own words and actions: "Stevens is playing the role of uncle, teaching his nephew ideals by which to live, and in the process, he naturally betrays the differences between what he thinks and what he fails to do" (43). Stevens's approach also seems inadequate in that it emphasizes the inescapable nature of history, exactly the influence from which Chick tries to escape. As the mob leaves the town square, Chick reflects on one of his uncle's speeches about the nature of time that specifically refers to Gettysburg:

> It's all *now*, you see. Yesterday wont be over until tomorrow and tomorrow began ten thousand years ago. For every Southern boy fourteen years old, not once but whenever he wants it, there is the instant when it's still not yet two oclock on that July afternoon in 1863, the brigades are in position behind the rail fence, the guns are laid and ready in the woods and the furled flags are already loosened to break out and Pickett himself with his long oiled ringlets and his hat in one hand probably and his sword in the other looking up the hill waiting for Longstreet to give the word and it's all in the balance, it hasn't happened yet, it hasn't even begun yet, it not only hasn't begun yet but there is still time for it not to begin against that position and those circumstances which made more men than Garnett and Kemper and Armstead and Wilcox look grave yet it's going to begin, we all know that, we have come too far with too much at stake and that moment doesn't need even a fourteen year old boy to think *This time. Maybe this time.* . . . (430-31)

Stevens's subsequent reference to the lines from the Djuna Barnes poem, "To the Dead Favourite of Liu Ch'e" illustrates his approach perfectly. He recalls the lines, "*the scattered tea goes with the leaves and every day a sunset dies*" and from them concludes, "yesterday's sunset and yesterday's tea both are inextricable from the scattered indestructible uninfusable grounds blown through the endless corridors of tomorrow, into the shoes we will have to walk in and even the sheets we will have ((or try)) to sleep between: because you escape nothing, you flee nothing" (*ID* 431). Stevens's reference to the "grounds blown through the endless corridors of tomorrow" sounds suspiciously, perhaps even deliberately, similar to his earlier description of the dust of the past. And Chick seems wise to challenge such inevitability through his actions because, as Thomas Carmichael points out, Stevens even misquotes Barnes by "omitting a line from between the two that he cites."[1] Carmichael adds, "Although Gavin Stevens cites this poem to substantiate his claim about the inescapability of the past, his allusion might well be read as an ironic gloss on his notion of inevitable repetition" (24).[2] Stevens essentially uses this poetic lament for someone lost forever to the passage of time, the speaker's, Liu Ch'e's, favored paramour to illustrate, most unsuitably, his notions about how one can never escape the past. Those who forget history may very well be doomed to repeat it, but a view of the past such as Stevens's can also have a paralyzing effect. Chick instinctively has a better grip on the potential for individual action than his uncle can ever hope to have. For some reason, perhaps simply because of his youth, the idea of the past does not trap Chick quite so fully as it does Stevens, and he defies it through a type of direct action that totally eludes his uncle.

Chick's burgeoning awareness seems even more significant given the political climate that existed as Faulkner composed the novel. In 1948, the Democratic National Convention became divided over the controversial civil rights planks added to its agenda. Thirty-five Southern democrats who refused to support Harry Truman walked out of the convention and formed a third party, the States' Rights Party, commonly referred to as the "Dixiecrats."[3] Faulkner adamantly believed that the South had a responsibility to resolve its own racial issues, so he agreed with the Dixiecrat position on states' rights, but he opposed their racist rhetoric. As he told an interviewer just before the 1948 presidential election: "I'd be a Dixiecrat myself if they hadn't hollered 'nigger.' I'm a States' Rights man" (*LG* 60). In *Intruder in the Dust*, Faulkner offers, through Chick, a more moderate (albeit impractical) solution to the racial problems of the day, one that favors individual action. In contrast to his uncle, who talks about abstract racial issues and the plight of blacks in the post-Civil War South but fails to take any sort of effective action, Chick sees a wrong and risks his very life to correct it. Furthermore, Chick seems far more sensitive than Stevens to the intrinsic humanity of all people, especially African Americans. For example, in stark contrast to his uncle's inability to understand Mollie's grief in the final pages of *Go Down, Moses*, Chick recognizes as a child that *"You dont have to not be a nigger in order to grieve"* after seeing Lucas just after Molly's death (*ID* 302). And Stevens even admits that he stands to learn much from Chick. When Chick returns from his overnight grave-digging adventure, Stevens asks of him, "When did you really begin to believe him [Lucas]? When you opened the coffin, wasn't it? I want to know, you see. Maybe I'm not too old to learn either. When was it?" (379). The final testament to Chick's growth appears in the novel's last pages. Lucas enters Stevens's office to offer payment and asks Chick, "You aint fell in no more creeks lately, have you?" Chick, for the first time, responds not with an attempt at one-upmanship prompted by shame, but instead replies in a light tone, "I'm saving that until you get some more ice on yours." Lucas's response, in turn, seems quite genuine as he tells Chick, "You'll be welcome without waiting for a freeze" (465). This small vignette, rather than Stevens's unsatisfying exchange with Lucas about debts owed and paid, seems the true climax of the novel, the pinnacle of Chick's understanding of his own past behavior as well as that of those around him.

In spite of Stevens's characteristically obtuse behavior in that final episode, Chick finally comes to the understanding that he demonstrates therein due to his uncle's influence. At the end of chapter nine, Stevens gives his nephew a bit of advice that he desperately needs to hear at the time. This moment occurs when Chick comes close to revealing accidentally his own selfish motives for involving himself in Lucas's predicament. Faulkner describes the great wave of shame that consumes Chick as he feels "the hot hard blood burn all the way up his neck into his face." Stevens, obviously recognizing something of what Chick feels, tells him that in addition to refusing to bear certain things, as he has already done, he should also "just regret" his past mistakes and not "be ashamed" of things which he cannot change now (*ID* 439). While Chick certainly still regrets this and probably other blunders, by the time of that climactic scene with Lucas he seems to have heeded his uncle's advice and learned to move beyond the shame that so crippled him when the novel began.

Some of Faulkner's more minor references to dust point to Chick as the novel's intruder as well. In the initial flashback scene, Chick enters Lucas's yard and describes it as "completely bare, no weed no sprig of anything, the dust each morning swept by some of Lucas' womenfolks" (*ID* 289). In some ways, dust seems to epitomize the general condition of Jefferson's African American population. Faulkner again makes reference to the "grassless treeless yards" of similar residences as Chick and his uncle drive to the exhumation (395), and Chick earlier noticed that he "had not seen one Negro" walking the "dusty roads" leading into town (355). Chick's observation implies, of course, that only the poorest of whites would have walked through the road's dust in a similar fashion, without even a mule to lift them above it. And, most obviously, the jail's inmate population consists of "five Negroes" incarcerated separately from Lucas in the "dusty glare" of Jefferson's jail (325).

As Chick intrudes into this world filled with the metaphorical dust, indeed the fallout generated by the intersection of race and history, Faulkner necessarily goes with him. From a modern standpoint, this incursion seems somewhat less than revolutionary. As Moreland observes, Faulkner's attempt to deal with racial issues in a contemporary fictional setting "includes more than its share of clumsiness and embarrassment" ("Faulkner's Continuing Education" 63). Moreland further suggests that "Faulkner's novel might be understood as reaching clumsily and hopefully" in a "cross-cultural direction" and adds that in it, Faulkner "may be trying to grasp a cultural and personal model some features of which he can appreciate and articulate from his position, but other features of which he may blur or distort under the pressure of his own needs or by imagining them in terms of more familiar models, models he might reject but cannot quite articulate his way beyond" (65).[4] Faulkner's delineation of Lucas likely presents the novel's most problematic element; after all, he hardly comes across as a radical figure. He epitomizes, as Dussere points out, "a version of the perfect Negro Faulkner invokes in his public writings, the one who is required to be *superior* to white people in order to be deserving of equality" (54). Such criticism, of course, seems obvious enough in the twenty-first century, but we cannot forget that, as a product of the 1940s, *Intruder in the Dust* bears these and many other marks of the era of its composition. Therefore it seems even more remarkable that Faulkner intrudes, however problematically, into the social and political situation of his own day by having Stevens voice theories about how the South might solve its racial dilemma through individual action, and then undercutting Stevens's inaction when two young boys and a spunky old lady do what Stevens only lectures about. Of course the fictional effort stands as a single occurrence, an isolated action, but as Chick comes to learn, change has to begin somewhere. Stevens predicts that "Someday Lucas Beauchamp can shoot a white man in the back with the same impunity to lynch-rope or gasoline of another white man; in time he will vote anywhen and anywhere a white man can and send his children to the same school anywhere the white man's children go and travel anywhere the white man travels as the white man does it. But it wont be next Tuesday" (*ID* 401). For once Stevens is right, despite his fatuousness, and in many ways we continue to wait for next Tuesday, although not in the simplistic sense that Stevens's statement implies. By depicting the possibilities inherent in Chick's experience, Faulkner takes us a bit closer to that day his fiction envisions, one when the dust might finally settle.

• CHAPTER FOUR •

"Justice as He Sees It": *Knight's Gambit* and *Requiem for a Nun*

I looked down at the chessboard. The move with the knight was wrong. I put it back where I had moved it from. Knights had no meaning in this game. It wasn't a game for knights.

—Philip Marlowe (Chandler 707)

Gavin Stevens acts misguidedly in *Intruder in the Dust* as in much of Faulkner's earlier work, and Faulkner increasingly demonstrates Stevens's capacity to cause very real, if perhaps inadvertent, damage as he develops and assumes a more central role in the fiction. Nowhere is that destructive potential more obvious than in *Requiem for a Nun*, a novel over which critics have exerted much energy in trying to reconcile Stevens's decidedly ambiguous actions with Faulkner's presumptive sympathy for him as a character. Mary Montgomery Dunlap voices an opinion it would seem that many would like to believe of Stevens's inaction in *Intruder in the Dust*: "He does not fail in kindness, but he does fail in comprehension" (44). Accordingly, the early readings of *Requiem* almost uniformly overlook Stevens's shortcomings in order to preserve untarnished sympathy for him. In one particularly glowing interpretation, Olga W. Vickery christens Stevens the "Sage of Yoknapatawpha" who "becomes a Socratic midwife presiding over the moral dialectic which focusses on Temple Drake. Like Plato's greater creation, his one saving grace in a thankless job is his awareness that he must humble himself to learn as well as to teach, to be led as well as to lead" (123). Michael Millgate similarly refers to Stevens as "the grand inquisitor of Faulkner's particular brand of humanism, at once leading and forcing Temple along the road towards what he believes to be her salvation" (*Achievement* 221). Such flattery leads Barbara Ladd to term the Gavin Stevens of the 1950s and early 60s a "kind of moral superman" (489). There are, of course, exceptions. Most notably, in 1952, Irving Howe referred to Stevens as "the greatest wind-bag in American literature" (286). John Lewis Longley, Jr. similarly mentions that Stevens frequently jumps to conclusions and talks too much (37).

Noel Polk points out, though, that such criticisms are "right, but for the wrong reasons." Because "too many people simply believe that everything Stevens says carries the weight of Faulkner's own convictions," critics generally treat such traits as weaknesses in Faulkner's writing, without "considering that this is part of Faulkner's deliberate characterization of him" (*Faulkner's Requiem* 55-56). Polk's revisionist approach to *Requiem* first questioned the validity of such genial interpretations; indeed, Polk points to the "dangerous potential for simple myopia in Stevens's concern for *justice as he sees it*" (*Faulkner's Requiem* 61). He views Stevens not as a saint but as just another character with an agenda that he presents in the guise of justice (66). Though some criticize Polk's re-envisioning of *Requiem* as overstated and excessively critical of Stevens, it nevertheless expands the potential of the text and complicates Stevens as a character.[1] Consequently, readings of Stevens and his motivations in this novel now run a gamut of possibilities, all of which turn upon intentionality. Most of the more positive readings weigh Stevens's actions against his intentions as they concern Temple; for example, Karl F. Zender feels that "the whole objective of Gavin Stevens's long struggle with Temple Drake is to have her tell the story of her life in a new way, one that will not renew her illicit memories but will instead purge her of them" ("*Requiem*" 277). Conversely many, mainly feminist, critics extend Polk's reading and accordingly take Stevens to task for his actions. For example, Ladd notes that although Stevens talks more than any other character about morality, Faulkner "places the moral imperative securely in the hands of a woman" in *Requiem* (491). Ladd demonstrates how, by eliciting Temple's confession, Stevens reprivatizes her into the novel's patriarchal framework of separate public and private spheres (488).[2] The debate comes down to several options; the most popular contention still views Stevens as Temple's savior, the one who finally forces her not only to face her past but also to deal with it in a practical way. A slightly less prevalent version admits that Stevens's obsessive pursuit of the truth might have actually made the situation worse but absolves (or at least rationalizes) Stevens's actions in light of his intentions.[3] Finally, Polk stands alone in aggressively questioning the purity of Stevens's motives:

> Part of what motivates Stevens in *Requiem*, I would suggest, is his horror at having in his family the eight-year-old scandal, as well as its more recent variation, and his desire to purge the family of it, or at the very least to dissociate himself from it in a public way. Perhaps this possibility is too speculative and oversubtle, and one clear objection to it is the question, if Stevens is horrified by the scandal, why does he not rather want to hush things up than to pursue them? Stevens, however, wants not merely to

exorcise but to punish; and, besides, who can tell what form a mania will take? (*Faulkner's* Requiem 66)

What form indeed? While his reading of Stevens as a self-interested individual differs radically from those preceding it, the possibility that Polk presents hardly seems "too speculative and oversubtle." In the earlier collection of detective stories, *Knight's Gambit*, Faulkner suggests that Stevens's evolving ideas about justice necessitate such a skeptical interpretation of both his character and his motivations. In the early stages of their collaboration on the unrealized play that *Requiem* grew out of, Faulkner wrote to Joan Williams, "She [Nancy] deserves to hang, a sentiment which reflects even on the lawyer defending her" (*SL* 298). The dimensions of that reflection, as well as its roots, lie within the pages of *Knight's Gambit*.[4]

Although *Knight's Gambit* and *Requiem for a Nun* might initially appear tenuously related, their textual histories intertwine in curious ways. Faulkner completed the first story featured in *Knight's Gambit*, "Smoke," in 1930 and *Harper's Bazaar* purchased and published it in 1932 (Blotner, *A Biography* [1984] 255, 297); then, in 1933, he tried to write two separate openings for a novel he intended to title *Requiem for a Nun*. Although few clues concerning the plot of that proposed novel exist, one of the openings features Stevens as a character (Polk, *Faulkner's* Requiem 237-45). Over a decade later in 1948, Faulkner heavily revised and expanded the short story "Knight's Gambit" into the novella that serves as the basis for the collection's title. Random House published the volume in 1949, and shortly thereafter in 1950 Faulkner made the first of many unsuccessful attempts to collaborate with Williams on the proposed play (Blotner, *A Biography* [1984] 512-13). The material for both pieces occupied Faulkner's mind if not concurrently, then at least in fairly close chronological proximity.

Most critics regard *Knight's Gambit* as one of Faulkner's minor texts, one much less important than *Requiem*. Even Michael Millgate, who speculates that the collection "has perhaps been too readily dismissed," deems the work one of only "minor importance" (*Achievement* 265).[5] As John F. Jebb points out, some scholars do offer praise for individual works, but "there is no critical consensus on which stories are impressive" (147). Millgate voices a fairly standard opinion when he speculates that Faulkner "was merely 'coasting' in these stories" (*Achievement* 267). Among those few critics who see some value in *Knight's Gambit*, prevailing issues include notions about the outsider's relationship to community and Faulkner's adaptation of the genre of detective fiction.[6] Most scholars feel that the volume's main worth, though, lies in its depiction of Stevens as an evolving character; indeed, Stevens is "twenty-eight" in the story Chick retroactively narrates in "Tomorrow" and "almost fifty" in the title novella (85, 238). Millgate observed early on, "The volume does have a certain thematic unity, and we can perceive in it some of the stages by which

Faulkner worked towards . . . his final conception of Gavin Stevens" (*Achievement* 265). *Knight's Gambit's* ultimate contribution, argues Millgate, "lies in its presentation of Gavin Stevens, who appears here [in the final novella, *Knight's Gambit*] as a more elaborately developed character and as a somewhat different one" (269-70).

Conceptions of truth and justice in the collection comprise a key, though largely unexplored, aspect of this evolution.[7] Before addressing those themes, though, it seems crucial to acknowledge that Faulkner utilizes the different terms for very specific ends. Truth (and its attendant counterpart, fact) and justice exist as slippery concepts in his fiction, much as they do in life. Truth seems the easiest of the three to define, mainly because Faulkner did so himself during one of his interviews in Nagano:

> Yes, truth to me means what you know to be right and just, truth is that thing, the violation of which makes you writhe at night when you try to go to sleep, in shame for something you've done that you know you shouldn't have done. That to me is truth, not fact. Fact is not too important and can be altered by law, by circumstance, by too many qualities, economics, temperature, but truth is the constant thing, it's what man knows is right and that when he violates it, it troubles him. Well, I doubt if he ever does toughen himself, toughen his soul, to where it doesn't trouble him just a little and he'll try to escape from the knowledge of that truth in all sorts of ways, in drink, drugs, various forms of anesthesia, because he simply cannot face himself. (LG 145)

Truth, then, for Faulkner, operates on an individual level akin to conscience. Truth stands for everything good and right, the way we think the world *should* be, and facts entail mere exigencies of particular situations. Faulkner's fiction illustrates the distance between the two and explores the ways people cope with the actions they take that violate truth as they see it. Faulkner suggests that one can alter facts to bring about this state of truth or use them to destroy it: truth, though, "is not an impossible dream" but "a quality which one must accept or cope with. That is, he must accept or spend all his life running from it" (145).

As complicated as that may sound, justice in Faulkner's work presents a far more difficult prospect, primarily because so little of it exists. In his analysis of these principles in *Knight's Gambit*, W.E. Schlepper determines that the "prerequisite for justice—no less than for retribution—is, of course, possession of the truth" (370). Schlepper apparently refers to a truth synonymous with fact, what actually happens, but his comment nevertheless poses some interesting questions: first, does justice mean the same thing as retribution? In *Requiem*, Gowan Stevens doesn't seem to think so. After returning home from Nancy's trial, he tells his uncle, Gavin Stevens, "I wish to God that what I wanted was only revenge. An eye for an eye—were ever words emptier? Only, you have got to have lost the eye to know it" (518). It later becomes painfully apparent that Gavin Stevens, who has lost nothing, does not, and perhaps cannot, know this. Schlepper's statement further begs the question of whether or not truth must actually precede justice. If so, what sort of truth? The kind of truth synonymous with fact that Schlepper refers to or Faulkner's individualized moral truth? Truth as fact seems hardly relevant to Temple who, in her zeal to save Nancy's life, exclaims to Stevens, "Truth? We're trying to save a condemned murdress whose lawyer has already admitted that he has failed. What has truth got to do with that?" (*RN* 532). As Polk points out, much of the debate in *Requiem* stems from Temple's and Stevens's conflicting ideas about what constitutes truth; Stevens "has identified 'truth' solely with the *facts* of Temple's past" (*Faulkner's* Requiem 89), whereas Temple "prefers to temper the full truth with the pity and courage that Stevens only talks about" (91). So, to use Faulkner's equation, Temple manipulates (or perhaps only elides) mere fact in an attempt to create her version of a higher truth, one relevant to her. Without delving any further than necessary into the thorny specifics of Faulkner's usage, we can, by extension, attribute a similar relativity to his concept of moral justice; like truth, it differs for each individual. Schlepper's painstaking attempt to define such amorphous terms as truth and justice, and his deduction that *Knight's Gambit* deals with "how, once the extreme of murder is resorted to, people endeavour to gain truth and approximate justice," assume that some great unitary ideal of truth or justice exists (375), when, for Faulkner's characters, it clearly does not. Such concepts necessarily remain individualized.

Therefore it comes as no surprise when Faulkner tells us that, for all his talk of truth, Stevens champions "not so much . . . truth" but "justice as he sees it" (*RN* 505-06). It does, however, seem remarkable that so many scholars consider this to be positive. For example, Vickery praises Stevens for reestablishing "justice as a moral and personal concept instead of merely a legal and social precept" (115) and Jebb more recently offered approval for Stevens's ability to translate "ideals about justice into real experience" (13). Why? Stevens practices law, sometimes as a prosecutor and sometimes as a defense attorney; the law should be his primary concern, not truth, or, for that matter, justice of the moral brand. The taxpayers of Yoknapatawpha County pay Stevens for dispensing *legal* justice, not morality. Moreover, by defending alleged criminals while acting as County Attorney, Stevens actually commits a serious breach of legal ethics. In "Hand Upon the Waters," when Stevens goes to the scene of Lonnie Grinnup's drowning, Faulkner notes that as "county attorney he [Stevens] had no business there" (65). In *Requiem*, Faulkner again mentions that Stevens frequently involves "himself, often for no pay, in affairs of equity and passion and even crime too among his people, white and Negro both, sometimes directly contrary to his office of County Attorney which he has held for years" (506). Stevens, then, problematically continues to serve as

County Attorney even as he defends Nancy. In *Politics in Mississippi*, Charles A. Marx and Thomas E. Payne write of the position:

> On the county level an elected county prosecutor serves as a prosecutor representing the state in all felony and misdemeanor cases up to the point in the case where it is bound over to the grand jury. The county prosecuting attorney can work closely with local and state law enforcement on criminal cases and the presentation of the case at preliminary hearings. (192)

Instead of pursuing the state's case, though, Stevens effectively joins the opposing team when he defends Nancy before the grand jury. Thus Faulkner delineates a doubly inappropriate situation in which Stevens defends a woman who murdered a member of his own family only after charging her with that crime. Stevens's actions surely violate the spirit, if not the actual letter, of the law.

Therefore, when critics praise Stevens for, as Hans H. Skei puts it, "seeing justice done, even if justice and truth are not always the same" ("Detection" 81), they must overlook that Stevens's position simply does not allow him the luxury of making such distinctions. As an officer of the court, Stevens's profession necessitates that he deal with Nancy's fate, not Temple's. Although he does distinguish between truth and the law, as when he explains to Nancy at her trial that her plea of not guilty "had nothing to do with truth but only with law" (*RN* 607), he fails to discriminate between legal justice and his ideas of what constitute it. As Leonard I. Kulseth notes, Stevens stands guilty of "sometimes putting his view of justice above the law" (29), or, as Faulkner might have said, Stevens often manipulates fact to create his version of truth and/or justice. Jebb takes note of this tendency and speculates that in *Requiem*, Stevens might focus on reforming Temple because he "may reason that because she [Nancy] is guilty, he can safely use her case to discover more about Temple; Nancy seems careless of what he does in her defense" (295). As Jebb recognizes, this rationale neglects the fact that Stevens has a professional obligation to provide Nancy the best defense possible, whether she cares if he does so or not.

In addition to the fact that Stevens ignores the most basic of his duties, his practice of creating this biased justice appears suspect because he clearly knows so little about people. As Cleanth Brooks observes, Maggie Mallison, Stevens's twin sister who knows him best, "loves her brother Gavin and is aware of his solid virtues, but she worries about the way in which he fails to see what women are like, and she finds him unable to understand humanity in general" ("Gavin Stevens" 31). Faulkner also told students at the University of Virginia that Stevens "knew a good deal less about people than he knew about the law and about ways of evidence" (*FU* 140), implying that Stevens knows more about legal justice than the other brand he feels compelled to construct.

Faulkner followed that comment with an even stronger indictment of Stevens, describing him as a "knight that goes out to defend somebody who don't want to be defended and don't need it" (141). In *Requiem*, Stevens defends (or at least he would likely call it that) Temple in this fashion, but, more importantly, he neglects Nancy, the very person he has pledged to legally defend and thus illustrates the dangers of self-made justice. Temple indirectly speaks to Stevens of this danger before she meets with Nancy for the last time:

> People. They're really innately, inherently gentle and compassionate and kind. That's what wrings, wrenches . . . . something. Your entrails, maybe. The member of the mob who holds up the whole ceremony for seconds or even minutes while he dislodges a family of bugs or lizards from the log he is about to put on the fire. . . . (652)

This passage directly follows Faulkner's extended description of the hymn, or "singing school" sessions that Stevens joins Nancy for nightly, an event that presents a particularly apt example of the dangers of self-made justice (649), the "humane" act that precedes Nancy's execution. Stevens does not know Nancy, nor does he try to; he instead judges her, sentences her through his inaction, holds her hand as she proceeds to the gallows, and, most importantly, forces Temple Drake to watch the whole sordid affair. Faulkner thought of Nancy as the nun of the title (*FU* 196), so perhaps Stevens's nightly ritual, the only musical performance in the text, serves as its requiem, a meaningless mass for the nearly-dead that serves only to commemorate the dangers of his manipulation.

Intentionality, then, provides no more accurate gauge of justice than morality does. The only measure Faulkner finally leaves us resides in the possibility that Stevens ignores: the law. Although in Jefferson, as in most places, the law does not even approach perfection, it nevertheless remains the best—and maybe the only—relatively objective, consistent measure of justice that exists. *Knight's Gambit* becomes a significant text, then, if for no other reason than that it charts a progressive move in Stevens's career away from endorsing impartial legal justice in favor of the self-made brand that he dispenses so recklessly in *Requiem*. During the planning stages of the collection, Faulkner considered two telling legal titles in a letter to Saxe Commins: "I haven't got a title yet. I think of something legal, perhaps in workaday legal Latin, some play on the word *res*, like *res in justicii* or *Ad Justicii*" (*SL* 287). The first possibility means "things decided" or "closed cases," and the second translates roughly as "toward justice."[8] This juxtaposition becomes significant in light of Stevens's growing propensity to manipulate justice to achieve his own questionable ends in the volume. Dunlap asserts that in *Knight's Gambit*, Stevens sees "justice as that which is fair in the human context rather than that which balances on the 'blind scales of justice'" (121); however, he does not initially assume such a subjective attitude. Stevens evolves as a character through a series of gradual shifts in his approach to justice. By the conclusion of the collection he progresses (or perhaps regresses) to endorsing not simply justice as he sees it but justice as it benefits him, thus setting the precedent for a similar approach in *Requiem*.

Stevens has little, if any, effect on the outcomes of the first two stories in *Knight's Gambit*. "Smoke," the initial work, describes a mystery within a mystery as it outlines the murders of both Anselm Holland and Judge Dukinfield, the jurist charged with validating his will. Granby Dodge, a cousin living with one of Holland's sons, eventually emerges as the culprit in this convoluted mystery. He hired a "thug" from Memphis to kill Anselm and planned to murder his son Virginius as well in an attempt to gain control of the family farm. The case, as Stevens presents it, turns upon the smoke of the title. During the inquest, Stevens establishes that the killer lit an unusual and easily recognizable brand of cigarette just after he shot Dukinfield. The judge's servant, Job, remembers smelling the smoke upon discovering the body, and he also recalls closing the small box that the judge used as a paperweight when it "jumped off the table" in the smoke-filled room (*KG* 32). Stevens proposes that if his theory holds true the box will still contain the unique smoke, and Dodge confesses when he jumps up and flaps "at the fading smoke" that emerges from the box when Stevens opens it (33).

Because of its implausibility, most critics consider "Smoke" the weakest component of the collection; Millgate even speculates that Faulkner included it only to "fill out what proved, even so, to be only a short book" (*Achievement* 265). The piece seems deliberately implausible, though, and occupies an undeniably significant position because it features Stevens's initial appearance as a character in Faulkner's published fiction. As such, it provides a crucial starting point for any analysis of Stevens. More importantly, it presents one of the most objective glimpses of him in the collection because Chick does not narrate it; rather, an unnamed juror hearing the case does so. This anonymous narrator initially criticizes Stevens by creating an unflattering dialectical comparison between him and Judge Dukinfield. He presents Dukinfield as a paragon of justice who holds the community's complete confidence: "we watched him without impatience, knowing that what he finally did would be right, not because he did it, but because he would not permit himself or anyone else to do anything until it was right" (*KG* 12). Dukinfield, the narrator says, "never had time to become confused and self-doubting with too much learning in the law" and knows that "justice is fifty per cent legal knowledge and fifty per cent unhaste and confidence in himself and in God" (11). Faulkner contrasts this epitome of common sense and small-town justice with Stevens, an intellectual (rather than practical) lawyer who possesses neither patience nor prudence. This characterization first becomes clear when

Stevens, facing the communal accusation that he used "unfair" methods to elicit Dodge's confession, flippantly replies, "But isn't justice always unfair? Isn't it always composed of injustice and luck and platitude in unequal parts?" (24).

Although this juror deems Stevens's methods questionable, more essentially, they appear merely unnecessary, a circumstance their implausibility emphasizes. Stevens already has two witnesses to the crime, the druggist, Doctor West, and Job, whose respective testimonies provide compelling circumstantial evidence (KG 27-31). However, even these witnesses become irrelevant in light of the hired assassin's confession as to who hired him and his admission of "where he had been" and "whom he had been to see" (29). When weighed against such evidence, the vapor of smoke wafting from the box at the story's climax, though quite dramatic, does not seem crucial to a conviction.[9] It does serve, however, to fuel Stevens's pride. As he tells Virginius about filling the box with the "incriminating" smoke a mere hour before the inquest, "something quick and eager" fills Stevens's eyes, and he speaks "quickly, brightly, cheerfully, almost happily" (35-36). This self-importance extends to his dealings with the family when he advises Virginius to "tear up" the will that named Dodge as an heir:

> 'Make Anse [his brother, not his father] your heir, if you have to have a will.'
> 'He won't need to wait for that,' Virginius said. 'Half of that land is his.'
> 'You just treat it right, as he knows you will,' Stevens said.
> 'Anse don't need any land.'
> 'Yes,' Virginius said. He looked away. 'But I wish. . . .'
> 'You just treat it right. He knows you'll do that.'
> 'Yes,' Virginius said. He looked at Stevens again. 'Well, I reckon I . . . we both owe you. . . .' (34) [10]

Virginius, who obviously considered splitting the land immediately with his brother in an attempt to mend broken familial fences, for some reason accedes to Stevens's opinion, advice that reflects Stevens's attitude of noblesse oblige and, moreover, presumes to impose Stevens's notions of how the world should operate upon a situation that really does not and should not concern him.

In addition to providing a valuable glimpse of Stevens through eyes other than Chick's, "Smoke" contains a significant indication of Stevens's initial view of himself as a jurist. Virginius remarks to Stevens, "When a man starts doing wrong, it's not what he does; it's what he leaves," and Stevens replies:

> But it's what he does that people will have to hurt him for, the outsiders. Because the folks that'll be hurt by what he leaves won't hurt him. So it's a good thing for the rest of us that what he does takes him out of their hands. I have taken him out of your hands now, Virge, blood or no blood. Do you understand? (KG 35)

For all of his needless showmanship, Stevens envisions himself as an impartial officer of the court, enforcing the justice that Virginius would not have had the wherewithal to pursue alone. Here, Faulkner gives us a point from which to measure Stevens's journey from legally sanctioned justice to "justice as he sees it" and thus gauge the distance between his initially detached interest and his personal entanglement in the legalities of *Requiem*.

Chick begins the second story, "Monk," by describing the tragic life of the title character, a mentally challenged orphan convicted of murder when his attorney, like Stevens in *Requiem*, fails to file the appropriate plea of mental incompetence (*KG* 39). Stevens eventually manages to secure a pardon for Monk, but by that time Monk has adjusted to the institutionalized routine of the penitentiary and developed great affection for the warden. Shortly after Monk declines the pardon, he stupefies Stevens by killing the warden whom he idolized with a "doglike devotion" (47). Stevens later discovers "by accident" that Monk murdered the warden at the inadvertent suggestion of another prisoner, Terrel. The tale's main action begins when the citizens of Yoknapatawpha County send Stevens as a delegate to protest the proposed gubernatorial pardon of Terrel and several other prisoners in what the governor himself describes as a ploy to garner votes in the upcoming election (50-54).

Faulkner gives us definite reason to doubt the strength of Stevens's commitment to seeing justice done when he walks out of the pardon board's hearing in a state of righteous indignation. As he drives through the Delta on his way back to Jefferson, he "was glad of the heat, he said; glad to be sweating, sweating out of himself the smell and the taste of where he had been" (*KG* 60). Jebb obviously thinks this sentiment representative of Faulkner's thinking and views Stevens as a "moral exemplar" in this story, "the only good man in a bleak, amoral setting" (155). Dunlap concurs and notes that for "all his efforts Stevens fails even to help achieve 'justice.' The villain is freed by a villainous, harshly opportunistic governor" (20). The governor may indeed have an opportunistic agenda; if so, he certainly would not be the first self-interested politician. However, if we adopt Stevens's righteous attitude toward him, we miss Faulkner's point and allow Stevens to fool us, along with himself, into thinking that the governor alone deserves blame. Stevens becomes at least as guilty as the governor through his inaction and evasion. When he faces the pardon board, comprised of "identical puppet faces," he does not even try to change the minds that he believes already made up. Why does he think the county sent him before the board? Certainly not to say, "No . . . I can't" and simply walk off into the purifying Delta heat (*KG* 59).

Moreover, Faulkner gives us reason to doubt Stevens's assessment of both Terrel's guilt and the governor's complicity. Terrel did not put Monk up to killing the warden; he seems distressed over Monk's execution, and as he says,

"I never told him to do nothing" (*KG* 58). Terrel might even stand equally innocent of the charge of manslaughter for which the state convicted him; the scant evidence, as Faulkner presents it, seems completely circumstantial, perhaps even flimsy (55-56). Stevens's denigration of Terrel's alibi and the guard's likening him to a "bad egg" hardly establish his guilt conclusively (58, 55), and Terrel seems pathetic rather than dangerous when he almost whimpers, "I just want justice. That's all" (57). Faulkner gives us definite reason to speculate that perhaps a wrongful, or at least an unsubstantiated conviction provides the impetus for the governor's offering Terrel a pardon. This also seems likely in that the governor does not totally lack morality. In his conversation with Stevens, the governor claims to have "principles," albeit of a different sort than those Stevens holds so dear:

> The Governor looked at him with an expression almost warm, almost pitying—and quite curious. 'Mr. Stevens, you are what my grandpap would have called a gentleman. He would have snarled it at you, hating you and your kind; he might very probably have shot your horse from under you someday from behind a fence—for a principle. And you are trying to bring the notions of 1860 into the politics of the nineteen hundreds. And politics in the twentieth century is a sorry thing, . . . smelling to high heaven in some-body's nose.' (54)

The governor obviously hails from a background less privileged than Stevens, one that does not afford him the luxury of such rigid morality. Yet he does not seem to be the completely amoral character that Stevens thinks him; he knows that the political environment in which he operates "is a sorry thing" and likely plays the political game as honestly as he can. He, like Temple, doubts humanity's potential, thinks that the twentieth century "stinks," as Temple might say. Thus he necessarily recognizes the impracticality of Stevens's absolutist ideals in the world of his political reality. While the governor hardly stands as a pillar of justice, he is by no means the villain that Stevens would have readers believe.

Stevens has a personal interest at stake in the volume's next two stories and accordingly takes a far more active role in both. In "Hand Upon the Waters," he abandons his objective approach to justice and involves himself in the case of Lonnie Grinnup's murder for a "sentimental reason" (*KG* 65). Grinnup, or "Grenier," descends, as does Stevens, from the "three simultaneous" pioneers who founded Yoknapatawpha County (66), hence the personal nature of Stevens's involvement. Stevens explains that because of his mental deficiencies, Louis Grenier has inadvertently re-christened himself "Lonnie Grinnup": "Louis Grenier, whose dead face Stevens was driving eight miles in the heat of a July afternoon to look at, had never even known he was Louis Grenier. He could not even spell the Lonnie Grinnup he called himself" (66). Stevens describes Grinnup as a poor "damned feeb" who lived at his river camp with Joe, another "deaf-and-dumb" man (65-66). Stevens eventually identifies Boyd Ballenbaugh as Grinnup's murderer and determines that Boyd's motive stems from the lure of easy money that Tyler's (his brother) policy insuring Grinnup's life presents. In the dramatic climactic scene, Boyd first shoots his brother and then Stevens but, at the last moment, Grinnup's partner, Joe, descends from his hidden perch in the trees and likely saves Stevens's life. Stevens wakes to find Boyd the victim of a violent death that Joe most certainly engineered; Joe admits as much by suspending the body from the same trotline that earlier held Grinnup (78-80).

Stevens finally metes out a form of self-made justice in this story, if only through inaction, by refusing to implicate Joe in Boyd's death. Even though the sheriff strongly suspects Joe's involvement and says as much to Stevens in his roundabout way, Stevens claims to have no memory of the events because, as he says, "I was shot, you see" (*KG* 80). Patrick Samway, S.J., asserts that Faulkner's resolution to "Hand" depicts, in "a sense," justice accomplished "without either a legal procedure or Gavin's intervention" ("Gavin Stevens" 155). In another sense, though, Stevens's omission does constitute a sort of intrusion with his deliberate refusal to confirm the sheriff's suspicions. Faulkner's title also suggests that Stevens thinks of his own behavior as a deliberate act, perhaps even one divinely inspired. The title alludes to Exodus 7:17, the verse in which God speaks to Moses of cursing the Egyptians with the plague of blood: "Thus saith the LORD, In this thou shalt know that I *am* the LORD: behold, I will smite with the rod that *is* in mine hand upon the waters which *are* in the river, and they shall be turned to blood." Verse 19 continues, "And the LORD spake unto Moses, Say unto Aaron, Take thy rod, and stretch out thine hand upon the waters of Egypt, . . . that they may become blood" (*King James Bible*). The intertextual connection seems straightforward enough, but Faulkner complicates it in interesting ways. Most obviously, it points to the key that first unlocks the mystery for Stevens, the paddle found in Grinnup's boat. Stevens realizes that Grinnup could not have died accidentally because he would never have used a paddle while baiting or checking a trotline. Stevens asks the Sheriff, "Didn't you ever run a trotline, a trotline right at your camp?" and points out that to do so, "You don't paddle, you pull the boat hand over hand along the line itself from one hook to the next. Lonnie never did use his paddle" (*KG* 81). The parallels Faulkner draws between this story and the passage from Exodus suggest that Stevens figuratively declines to use the paddle as well. In those verses, God appropriates Aaron's hand as his own when he declares that he will "smite" the waters with the rod "that *is* in mine hand," thus turning them to blood. Stevens thinks of himself as doing much the same thing, only through inaction. Rather than smiting the waters, so to speak, Stevens holds back the other bit of knowledge connected to his own "rod," the paddle, when he refuses to implicate Joe in Boyd's death. Stevens knows exactly which pair of hands killed Boyd; the last image he registers before blacking out is of Joe jumping from the trees with his "hands already extended" in preparation to attack Boyd (79). Stevens withholds this information because he deems murder a just punishment for a murderer, and in doing so he assumes a godlike responsibility for both Joe's life and Boyd's death.

Stevens's reservation, though, does not necessarily create justice, especially in light of the possible long-term effects. Jerome F. Klinkowitz feels that Stevens's level of personal involvement in "Hand" makes it "a more satisfying story" than those before it (89), but Faulkner also suggests that this personal interest actually clouds Stevens's judgment. Stevens fancies that he creates justice by withholding the information; however, Faulkner undercuts such a notion by presenting Joe as a potential Monk, another accident just waiting to happen with his mental deficiencies and similarly doglike devotion to Grinnup.[11] If Joe kills again while under the influence of someone less benevolent than Grinnup, Stevens will bear full responsibility. Stevens obviously ascribes to a biblical belief in retribution in this tale and thinks that "Justice" and "Lonnie Grinnup" want an "eye for an eye and tooth for a tooth" (KG 77). His omission allows him to envision himself delivering such retribution, but he fails to consider the dangers inherent in such an action.

Faulkner curiously places the next tale, "Tomorrow," quite late in the collection, even though he reveals the main action as a flashback to the first case that Stevens ever tried. Although Stevens tried the case years before, Chick retells the story of it in the narrative present. The narration, more than the story itself, presents a further evolution of Stevens's ideas about justice. Stevens tells Chick of that initial case, the only one "in which he was convinced that right and justice were on his side, that he ever lost" (KG 85). Critics almost invariably interpret the exchange as a lesson in the triumph of moral justice over law.[12] In this case, Stevens defends a farmer from Frenchman's Bend, named only as Bookwright, who freely admits to killing Buck Thorpe, a thoroughly unlikable man whom Faulkner identifies as "a brawler, a gambler, known to be a distiller of illicit whiskey and caught once on the road to Memphis with a small drove of stolen cattle" (86). Bookwright apparently shot this unsavory character to prevent him from eloping with his daughter. Although Stevens anticipates an easy acquittal (86), the jury fails to free him because of a lone holdout. Stevens identifies Jackson Fentry as the holdout by sending Chick to spy on the closed deliberations at Mrs. Rouncewell's boardinghouse. Before Chick leaves, Stevens tries to justify such deception. He tells Chick that "justice is accomplished lots of times by methods that won't bear looking at" (88-89), but the illegal—even outrageous— surveillance does not create justice, it merely satisfies Stevens's curiosity.

Stevens pursues the matter by interviewing Fentry's neighbors; he finally learns that Fentry has refused to acquit Bookwright because Thorpe was once "Jackson and Longstreet Fentry," a child Jackson Fentry took in after the boy's mother (a Thorpe) died in childbirth. Fentry devoted himself to the child and did everything for him; his neighbor, Mrs. Pruitt, says, "It was like he even begrudged the earth itself for what that child had to eat to keep alive" (*KG* 95). Over two years later, the Thorpe family shows up to claim the child, saying only, "He is our kin. We want him and we aim to have him" (101). Fentry gives the boy up only after Isham Quick tells him, "It's the law, Jackson" (103).

This first trial, as Stevens presents it to Chick, looks like another case of retributive justice: the law takes the child from Fentry, and Fentry later uses the law to prevent Thorpe's killer from going free. At least Stevens understands it as such and tells Chick, "Of course he wasn't going to vote Bookwright free" (*KG* 104). When Chick replies, "I would have freed him. Because Buck Thorpe was bad," Stevens voices the alleged lesson in morality that he wants Chick to learn:

> 'No, you wouldn't,' Uncle Gavin said. He gripped my knee with one hand even though we were going fast, the yellow light beam level on the yellow road, the bugs swirling down into the light beam and ballooning away. 'It wasn't Buck Thorpe, the adult, the man. He [Fentry] would have shot that man as quick as Bookwright did, if he had been in Bookwright's place. It was because somewhere in that debased and brutalized flesh which Bookwright slew there still remained, not the spirit maybe, but at least the memory, of that little boy, that Jackson and Longstreet Fentry, even though the man the boy had become didn't know it, and only Fentry did. And you wouldn't have freed him either. Don't ever forget that. Never.' (104-05)

Stevens's instruction sends a far different message concerning his ideas about justice. Jebb contends that "law and justice collide" in "Tomorrow" (177), as they probably do in Chick's memory; however, the facts of the case imply that those two concepts actually remain far apart. An examination of the story from a standpoint removed from Chick's rosy memories reduces the whole of it to a perversion of the legal system rather than a triumph of moral justice. In addition to having Chick spy on the jury's deliberations, Stevens fails to provide any sort of viable legal defense for Bookwright. His sole strategy consists of displacing blame. The inexperienced Stevens seems incapable of mounting an adequate defense after he persuades his grandfather, Judge Stevens, to let him handle the case alone. Indeed, Judge Stevens only gives the case to Stevens, who is "twenty-eight" and "only a year out of the state-university law school," because "everybody believed the trial would be a mere formality" (*KG* 85). At trial Stevens contends, most unreasonably, that Bookwright took the only action he could since the community "didn't know in time" to prevent his crime; in the absence of such communal support, Stevens argues, Bookwright "solved that problem to the best of his ability and beliefs" (87, 88). Judge Stevens, obviously recognizing the inadequacy of this defense, remarks, "Well, Gavin, at least you stopped talking in time to hang just your jury and not your client" (88). It seems clear that Fentry refuses to acquit Bookwright of killing Thorpe because of their history, though, not because of Stevens's defense tactics.

After learning of Fentry's connection to Thorpe, Stevens sympathizes with Fentry's refusal as a tragic attempt to create some form of justice for himself; however, Fentry's idea of justice may actually come closer to generating impartial legal justice than Stevens's actions, although Fentry surely stands firm for other reasons. Fentry refuses to pardon the man who killed his would-be son to prevent him from marrying the Bookwright girl. Granted, we know little about the circumstances of the shooting, only that Thorpe supposedly "had a pistol in his hand when they found him" (*KG* 89) and that Bookwright confessed after he "waked Will Varner, the justice of the peace and the chief officer of the district, and handed Varner his pistol and said, 'I have come to surrender. I killed Thorpe two hours ago'" (86). Therein lies Faulkner's point: no one bothers to investigate the crime, and Fentry's refusal to acquit Bookwright prevents the jury from setting the man free simply because they think him a good man, as Chick puts it, "a solid, well-to-do farmer, husband and father, too" (85).

The more important message, then, in Stevens's discussion of the case with his nephew concerns his capacity for bending the rules and condoning, if not yet actively dispensing, justice as he sees fit even this early in his legal career. "Tomorrow" provides a glimpse of upcoming perversions of legal justice that occur when Stevens's judgment fails because his interests lie elsewhere. Stevens thinks of Fentry, much as he will come to regard Temple in *Requiem for a Nun*, as one of the "lowly and invincible of the earth" destined to "endure and endure and then endure, tomorrow and tomorrow and tomorrow" (*KG* 104). This perception also colors Stevens's retrospective explanation of the case to Chick, and, by extension, explains why he judges Thorpe deserving of murder at Bookwright's hand but fails to think Bookwright could be similarly accountable. To be clear, Stevens fulfills his obligations to Bookwright in his representation of him, but he obviously thinks Bookwright a good man, one worthy of life, and sees Thorpe as an amoral abomination. This belief probably sparks Stevens's desire to represent Bookwright in the first place. At the very least, Stevens thinks Jefferson a better place without Thorpe, and that belief undoubtedly informs the acquittal he secures the following spring.

In the final two stories of *Knight's Gambit*, Stevens fully evidences the self-interested approach to justice that defines his actions in *Requiem*. "An Error in Chemistry" elucidates Stevens's notions of truth and justice via Chick's summary of a discussion between Stevens and the sheriff:

> 'I'm interested in truth,' the sheriff said.
> 'So am I,' Uncle Gavin said. 'It's so rare. But I am more interested in justice and human beings.'
> 'Ain't truth and justice the same thing?' the sheriff said.
> 'Since when?' Uncle Gavin said. 'In my time I have seen truth that was anything under the sun but just, and I have seen justice using tools and instruments I wouldn't want to touch with a ten-foot fence rail.' (KG 111)

Stevens considers the sheriff's assumption that truth should approximate justice simplistic, but the sheriff's belief actually seems more ideologically sound than Stevens's ambiguous dichotomy. Ideally, truth should produce justice, or at least something close to it; our nation's legal system is predicated on that precept. The sheriff, perhaps Faulkner's most palatable lawman, does not quite buy Stevens's distinction. Later, he openly denigrates it when he tells Stevens that the homicide victim of their current case, Joel Flint's wife, "wasn't important enough for even that justice you claim you prefer above truth, to avenge her" (119).

This story, surely the most conventional in the collection, won second place in a contest sponsored by *Ellery Queen Mystery Magazine*, a circumstance that irked Faulkner considerably.[13] It features Flint as a one-time carnival man and master of disguise inauspiciously hiding out in Jefferson. He abandons that obscurity by killing his wife and father-in-law in order to gain control of the valuable clay lying just beneath the ground of their farm. After committing the murders, Flint brazenly impersonates his father-in-law, Old Man Pritchel, and summons the sheriff and Stevens to the farm, effectively daring them to discover his deception. They do uncover Flint's plot, though, largely because of his arrogant assumptions of invincibility. Everyone in Jefferson knows of Flint's predilection for drinking his whiskey straight, so when, disguised as Pritchel, he attempts to mix a cold toddy such as the old man favored, he makes the grievous mistake of trying to mix sugar with whiskey and exposes himself. As Chick says, "even I knew that to make a cold toddy you do not put the sugar into the whiskey because sugar will not dissolve in raw whiskey but only lies in a little intact swirl like sand at the bottom of the glass" (KG 127). Stevens says of the vanity that led to Flint's downfall: "What else could the possession of such a gift as his have engendered, and the successful practising of it have increased, but a supreme contempt for mankind? You [the sheriff] told me yourself that he had never been afraid in his life" (131). In other words, Flint would likely have escaped if not for his compulsion to show off. The sheriff admits that he would have done "Nothing" even if he and Stevens had discovered Pritchel's badly mutilated body in the barn and thought it Flint's (130). Flint's supposition that he lives beyond the reach of the law leads directly to his capture, and critics generally accept this circumstance as

Faulkner's lesson to Flint concerning the consequences of pride.[14] An exchange between Stevens and the sheriff suggests that the warning equally applies to Stevens:

> 'Yes,' the sheriff said. 'The Book itself says somewhere, *Know thyself*. Ain't there another book somewhere that says, *Man, fear thyself, thine arrogance and vanity and pride?* You ought to know; you claim to be a book man. Didn't you tell me that's what that luck-charm on your watch chain [his Phi Beta Kappa key] means? What book is that in?'
> 'It's in all of them,' Uncle Gavin said. 'The good ones, I mean. It's said in a lot of different ways, but it's there.' (131)

The sheriff implies that Stevens should take his own advice concerning the dangers of pride, a lesson "said" several "different ways" throughout *Knight's Gambit*. Through the sheriff, Faulkner warns against the sort of pride that Stevens's Phi Beta Kappa key represents, an object that he sometimes touches while pondering a case.[15] Stevens believes that he possesses, as Flint does, a "gift" that others lack, the ability to create situations, illusions of a sort, which manufacture a version of justice based in his interpretation of case evidence. As Stevens solves the small-town mysteries detailed within the pages of this collection, he, again like Flint, comes to think his judgment infallible; the totality of his confidence becomes eminently clear in the concluding novella, "Knight's Gambit."

The title story reveals a rare personal glimpse of Stevens's life, rather an uncommon element in detective fiction. It opens with Stevens and Chick playing a game of chess when Melisandre Backus Harriss's children suddenly storm in, interrupt the game, and ask that Stevens use his position as county attorney to help them deport Captain Gualdres, Melisandre's guest whom Max Harriss describes as a "fortune-hunting Spick" out to marry her for money (*KG* 137). Readers later discover that each sibling also has an individual agenda: the unnamed daughter loves Gualdres herself, and Max hates him because Gualdres "always beat him. At everything" (181). Stevens does involve himself in the affair, though not on the terms the Harriss children dictate, because he has an agenda of his own that becomes clear only when, near the conclusion, Faulkner reveals that Melisandre and Stevens almost married some twenty years earlier (235).

In "Knight's Gambit," Stevens does not solve a crime so much as he prevents one from occurring after he discovers that Max has purchased Rafe McCallum's unmanageable stallion, a horse "said to have killed two men" (*KG* 201). When McCallum tells Stevens that he delivered the stallion to the "little stable" at the Harriss estate (211), Stevens surmises that Max plans to eliminate Gualdres by replacing the mare that he usually rides at night with the killer stallion. Faulkner made clear in a letter to Saxe Commins that

Stevens prevents the crime out of purely personal motivations: "It is a love story, in which Stevens prevents a crime (murder) not for justice but to gain (he is now fifty plus) the childhood sweetheart which he lost 20 years ago" (*SL* 280). Essentially, Stevens convinces Gualdres to take a rigged bet; as Chick says, "You bet him the girl. That he didn't want to cross that lot and open that stable door. And he lost" (*KG* 218). He does indeed lose, yet scholars largely excuse Stevens's manipulation. For example, John T. Irwin likens Stevens to a knight "who in one move was able to carry out his public duty by preventing a murder and at the same time accomplish the most personal of goals, the winning of a wife" ("Knight's Gambit" 115). Schlepper likewise thinks that justice triumphs in "Knight's Gambit" and notes that Stevens's prevention of Gualdres's murder pairs inversely with "An Error in Chemistry" in that "it shows the characters as human beings at such close range and in such detail that the potential murder is for once anticipated and, with luck, . . . prevented" (370).

Justice certainly prevails *for Stevens*, but the people he manipulates to achieve such justice hardly fare so well. Dunlap speculates that perhaps "the children are what hinder Gavin Stevens from acting" upon his feelings for Melisandre immediately after Harriss's death (87). She further speculates that he uses "methods that won't bear looking at" to remove them from the picture by "arranging a marriage for which one partner has no desire and forcing a young boy to enlist in the army" (96). Even with this criticism, though, Dunlap glosses over the legal ramifications of Stevens's manipulations. The Harriss children approach Stevens in a professional capacity; as Max says, "You're the Law here, aren't you?" (*KG* 137). Stevens, however, shuns legal action from the beginning. When the girl returns alone to Stevens's office and attempts to explain Max's hatred for Gualdres and the very real threat that he poses to him, Stevens pretends to misunderstand her wishes and disingenuously wonders why she wants him to "lock him [her brother] up." She replies, "Lock him up how? . . . I know that much about law, myself: that you cant keep anybody locked up just because of what they are planning to do" (179). While Stevens could not have arrested Max, he might have proposed something more reasonable. Instead, Stevens, in keeping with his actions in *Requiem*, approaches the affair as a game. He deliberately imposes such a metaphor on the situation by setting up a single chess problem for Chick as the Harriss girl exits and remarking, "Nothing by which all human passion and hope and folly can be mirrored and then proved, ever was just a game" (192).[16] And this serious game has devastating consequences for everyone but Stevens. He forces Max Harriss, as Max puts it, to "Enlist, or else" on the eve of World War II, an event looming on the horizon and likely responsible for Max's refusal to register for the draft (224-25). Nor can Stevens claim ignorance of what he sentences Max to; he served in WWI himself (though perhaps he spent most of it working as a Y.M.C.A. secretary) and remembers the spring of 1919 as "a garden at the end of a four-year tunnel of blood and excrement and fear in which that whole generation of the world's young men lived like frantic ants" (231).[17] Similarly, Melisandre's daughter and Gualdres meet with equally dismal fates. Gualdres does not merely resist the marriage, he goes so far as to tell Stevens, "In my country, the campo, there is a saying: Married; dead" (227). He then refers to Stevens as "a very dangerous man" and declares, "I do not like you" (228). Stevens later learns from Chick that Gualdres also joined the American army, most likely in an effort to escape his new wife, when Gualdres sends the simple message to him via Chick, "Now maybe you're satisfied" (243). And Stevens undoubtedly knows the sort of life that he dooms Gualdres to by arranging the marriage; he tells Chick that in Melisandre's daughter, Gualdres "got something this time a good deal more efficient and fatal than just an insane horse" (229).

Max and Gualdres, however, did not always fare so poorly. Comparing Stevens's various manipulations in "Knight's Gambit" with the corresponding situations in the short story that Faulkner began almost a decade earlier reveals a marked change in Faulkner's conception of Stevens's character. Most obviously, the Stevens of the earlier "Knight's Gambit" does not force Max to enlist against his wishes; the draft board has already drawn Max's number before he appears on Stevens's doorstep (*Manuscripts* 308). In this version it seems that Stevens, rather than damning Max to endure the horrors of war, saves him from the even worse fate of jail. After a grateful Max thanks him for preventing the murder, Stevens asks, with his tongue firmly in his cheek, "Even a draft army will be a little better than jail, wont it?" (324).

After Max leaves, Melisandre's daughter and Gualdes (Faulkner later added the "r") enter, excited about their plans for the future. Gualdes seems quite happy about his marriage and even happier about being a U.S. citizen when he observes, "Since three days ago, I am . . . a United States" (*Manuscripts* 325). In response to his newly found patriotism, Gualdes plans to enlist in the U.S. cavalry as soon as he and his new bride return from their honeymoon. Thus instead of dooming the Argentine captain to a fate equivalent to death, Stevens facilitates a marriage between Gualdes and a woman who truly loves him (319). In fact, Stevens apparently fails to manipulate Gualdes at all in the earlier version, even in the climactic scene at the stable. While the two men do engage in a bet, Faulkner here casts a very different light upon its outcome, primarily in that Gualdes seems far more capable than his counterpart in the novella. In the finished novella, the captain never enters the paddock; Rafe McCallum opens the stable door and single-handedly subdues the "screaming" stallion (*KG* 219-21). In the short story, however, Faulkner does not even mention McCallum in this scene, and Gualdes carries out his actions. Although Gualdes still expresses skepticism as he and Stevens near the stable, he nevertheless approaches the horse fully prepared to defend himself with his weighted crop, remarking, "I am not a fool" (*Manuscripts* 321). Gualdes proves as much when he calmly stands the horse down. Faulkner employs virtually the same heroic language to describe both scenes, and Chuck (who later evolves into Chick) notes that Gualdes, like McCallum, "never did run, he just walked, his back to the stallion until it was within ten feet of him" (323). After Gualdes climbs over the fence, Stevens remarks, "You lost" (323), and Gualdes replies, "Your pardon, . . . I won" (324). This exchange differs significantly from the corresponding one in the novella:

> 'I have lost,' Captain Gualdres said.
> 'Not lost,' his uncle said.
> 'Truth,' Captain Gualdres said. 'Not lost.' (*KG* 221)

In the earlier version of the story, Faulkner allows Gualdes to define his own experience, and the revision implies that a vast gulf exists between "winning" and "not losing." In the short story, Gualdes wins in that he masters the horse that could have ended his life, marries a devoted and wealthy young woman, and becomes the proud citizen of a country that he already loves enough to fight for. In the novella, he simply manages not to lose his physical life, though he sees the existence Stevens arranges for him as meaningless, a sort of living death.

In addition to portraying the Stevens of the initial "Knight's Gambit" as less manipulative, Faulkner makes him sympathetic in other ways. Most obviously, Stevens becomes a victim of circumstance when Melisandre marries Harriss in his absence. In the novella, Stevens rejects Melisandre and has only himself to blame for her marriage, but in the short story, expediency forces Melisandre to wed Harriss despite her betrothal to Stevens. When her father dies unexpectedly, she must act quickly to pay the mortgage, and marrying Harriss becomes her only option. As Chuck observes, "she had to marry Mr Harriss to save their plantation" (*Manuscripts* 303). Stevens's normally detached facade cracks when he reacts to this loss, and even Chuck can see that the pain of losing Melisandre "was in his eyes now." Faced with Melisandre's rejection, Stevens pursues his legal career and finds the human interaction that he craves "not in his office but on the galleries of country stores about the county." Faulkner tellingly notes that Stevens listens to people's troubles, "not, as he said, because he was interested in truth but because he was interested in justice" (304). Stevens's pursuit of simple justice, not justice as he sees it or justice as it benefits him, speaks to the gulf that separates the Stevens of the initial "Knight's Gambit" from the Stevens of the later novella. Faulkner might have recycled the story's title, but he altered his knight considerably between versions.

Stevens's increasingly deleterious manipulation of justice in *Knight's Gambit* casts a very different light upon the claim he makes at the close of the volume, "I have improved" (246). He has instead developed the boundless confidence in his abilities and judgment that leads him to manipulate Nancy's and Temple's respective fates to his own ends in *Requiem*. Just after she meets with the governor, Temple says to Stevens that Nancy, "the nigger, the dope-fiend whore, didn't hesitate to cast the last gambit—and maybe that's the wrong word too, isn't it?" Temple, however, chooses precisely the right word; she just mistakenly thinks that Nancy has cast it. Stevens actually does that when he plays God with Nancy's life in an effort, as Temple puts it, to make good "come out of evil" (*RN* 612). And Nancy makes it clear that she requires no more, that she actually expects Stevens to sacrifice her when she likens God to "a man that's got too many mules" and turns them loose to fend for themselves (658). Nancy says that God can, at most, give "you the chance. He gives you the best He can think of, that you are capable of doing." When you fail, as you inevitably will when you "run free in mule sin and mule pleasure," God "will save you" (659). Because Nancy *expects* life to kick her in the teeth, she makes it easy for Stevens to do so, and she does not even ask that he try to obtain any sort of earthly salvation for her. God did not help her, so why should Stevens? She only wants him to join her in praising the God that she has to believe will save her in the next life despite his failure to do so in this one. Thus she embraces, even welcomes, the familiarity of a death she and Stevens both believe she deserves, one that her God (the holder of too many mules) sanctions because, as Nancy puts it, she "can work" in the next life just as she has in this one (659).

Temple offers little more resistance when Stevens, as Diane Roberts observes, "co-opts and reconstructs her past to insist that her degradation was her own fault" thus forcing her into a "'Christian' altruism" (221), one not too far removed from Nancy's vision of herself as martyr. The passage in which Stevens gambles for Melisandre's hand provides a useful gloss on Stevens's misinterpretation of Temple. It begins when Stevens and Gualdres discuss the nearly blind thoroughbred mare that Gualdres continues to train by teaching her to jump at night. He says, "I teach her the—how you say it?—faith." Stevens replies, "I think the word you want is invulnerability" (*KG* 217), a concept differing drastically from faith. Faith entails trust, belief, and especially doubt, values extraneous to invulnerability. In much the same fashion, Stevens misconstrues Gualdres as a man who imagines himself similarly invincible, who believes only in his "destiny" as opposed to the less appealing, more determined concept of fate. Stevens presumes that Gualdres "doesn't believe in a fate. He doesn't even accept one," and, in response, arranges the "fate" of marriage for him. Stevens then refuses to believe that Gualdres truly loses the bet because he gains "A princess [Melisandre's daughter] and half a castle [the

Harriss fortune], against some of his bones and maybe his brains too" (218). Moreover, Stevens makes Gualdres agree with him:

> 'I have lost,' Captain Gualdres said.
> 'Not lost,' his uncle said.
> 'Truth,' Captain Gualdres said. 'Not lost.' Then Captain Gualdres said, 'Thanks.' (221)

Stevens effectively sabotages Gualdres and makes him thank him for it, and he does much the same thing with Temple. She first approaches Stevens seeking justice for Nancy; she wants him to plead insanity after the fact, to draw up a "sworn affidavit that this murdress was crazy when she committed the crime" (*RN* 530), certainly a reasonable defense even after the fact. She then lets Stevens manipulate her, by means of her intense guilt, into not just allowing him to pursue, but into *helping* him pursue, what the sheriff in "An Error in Chemistry" terms "that justice you [Stevens] claim you prefer" (*KG* 119). In the process, he somehow convinces her that she bears the blame for her child's death because she failed to foresee the impossible. Temple confirms her feelings of guilt when she says to the governor:

> Uncle Gavin was only partly right. It's not that you must never even look on evil and corruption; sometimes you cant help that, you are not always warned. It's not even that you must resist it always. Because you've got to start much sooner than that. You've got to be already prepared to resist it, say no to it, long before you see it; you must have already said no to it long before you even know what it is. (*RN* 563)

Stevens quite obviously believes that Temple deserves to suffer, and she yields so fully to his interpretation of her character that, by the time she speaks with Nancy, she can hardly separate her will from his. First she tells Nancy, "We–I thought that all I would have to do would be to come back and go to the Big Man and tell him that it wasn't you who killed my baby, but I did it eight years ago that day when I slipped out the back door of that train." A few sentences later she reverses the construct when she says, "Then *I–we* thought that all it would be was, for me just to come back here and tell you you had to die" (emphasis added, 656). Stevens's final gambit, then, brings about devastating results; he essentially ends Nancy's life and destroys Temple's will along with any scrap of self-worth she might have managed to hold on to, all in the name of truth, for the sake of what he calls justice.

Stevens's actions in *Knight's Gambit* foreshadow his behavior in *Requiem*, but the collection's title also calls attention to the evolution of Stevens's theory of justice and suggests that, in *Requiem*, he might pursue not simply justice as he sees it, but justice as it benefits him, in this case his need to know the truth about what happened to Temple Drake. In *The Mansion*, Charles reveals that Stevens would do almost anything to satisfy his overwhelming curiosity:

> Uncle Gavin always said he was not really interested in truth nor even in justice: that all he wanted was just to know, to find out, whether the answer was any of his business or not; and that all means to that end were valid, provided he left neither hostile witnesses nor incriminating evidence. Charles didn't believe him; some of his methods were not only too hard, they took too long; and there are some things you simply do not do even to find out. But his uncle said that he, Charles, was wrong: that curiosity is another of the mistresses whose slaves decline no sacrifice. (638)

The "gambit" of the title that Stevens employs to obtain this information derives from the Italian "gambretto," literally the act of tripping up. A gambit in chess functions as a tricky opening move in which a player sacrifices a minor piece in order to gain a better position, such as the move Stevens makes when he feeds Chick "the pawn which only he, Charles, seemed to have believed that nobody had forgotten about, and he moved and then his uncle moved and then as usual it was all over" (KG 176). Stevens similarly sacrifices what he sees as the minor players, Melisandre's children and Gualdres, for his own happiness much as he sacrifices Nancy and Temple in *Requiem*.

A useful connection and possible source for Faulkner's metaphor exists in Raymond Chandler's *The Big Sleep*, the basis for a screenplay that Faulkner worked on in late 1944 (Blotner, *A Biography* [1984] 460-62).[18] In the novel, Philip Marlowe, Chandler's detective, always keeps a chessboard with a problem laid out on it in his apartment. At one point, when his client's daughter, Carmen Sternwood, tries to seduce him, he observes, "There was a problem laid out on the board, a six-mover. I couldn't solve it, like a lot of my problems. I reached down and moved a knight" (705). A few pages later he reflects, "I looked down at the chessboard. The move with the knight was wrong. I put it back where I had moved it from. Knights had no meaning in this game. It wasn't a game for knights" (707). The line perhaps stuck with Faulkner; his knight certainly occupies a similarly precarious position. After all, no such move as a knight's gambit exists, a circumstance providing further evidence that Stevens, as a mere knight, has no business making the sorts of decisions that he does; Faulkner stops short of making him a king for a reason. By the end of *Knight's Gambit* and throughout *Requiem*, Faulkner tells us, in a multiplicity of ways, that life becomes a dangerous game indeed when errant knights such as Stevens play it. His terrifying truth and sliding scale of moral justice unfairly rig it to checkmate legal justice, the very precept that he, as a lawyer, simply must place above all else if he ever hopes to create justice that we can see too.

• CHAPTER FIVE •

"The Poet's Romantic Dream": Sir Gawain, Sir Galwyn of Arthgyl, and Stevens in the Snopes Trilogy

> The end of wisdom is to dream high enough not to lose the dream in the seeking of it.
>
> —William Faulkner (*FD* 597)

Given Faulkner's well-known love for the works of Miguel de Cervantes, *Don Quixote* seems the most obvious influence on his conception of Gavin Stevens (*FU* 50, 145, 150); Faulkner even likened Stevens and Quentin Compson to Don Quixote during one of his lectures at the University of Virginia (141). However, Marta Powell Harley also points to *Sir Gawain and the Green Knight* as the early text "most significantly reflected in Faulkner's works" (111).[1] Although Faulkner's fiction draws on a variety of myths, he exhibits a pointed interest in the character of Gawain.[2] In fact, he even christens two of his "knights," Sir Galwyn of Arthgyl and Stevens, with derivatives of Gawain's name.[3] Together, these two characters practically span the breadth of Faulkner's career; Galwyn appears in the apprentice piece, *Mayday*, and Stevens continues to develop significantly throughout much of the later fiction, most visibly in the last two books of the Snopes trilogy.[4] Both characters exhibit qualities of failed idealists and they have much in common; nevertheless, they operate with two very different philosophies and make radically different choices. An examination of the two figures in light of their relationship to *Sir Gawain and the Green Knight* highlights an aspect of the evolution of idealism in Faulkner's fiction and provides additional clues as to how we might continue to evaluate the evolving role that Faulkner assigns Stevens in the later fiction.[5]

Faulkner originally created *Mayday* as a courtship gift for Helen Baird. The 43-page manuscript, one of the hand-lettered booklets he crafted during the 1920s, finally surfaced in New Orleans in the private collection of William B.

Wisdom.[6] Calvin S. Brown echoes a fairly standard opinion when he describes it as "a lightly allegorical medieval pastiche" that "is no disgrace to Faulkner" (632). The critical efforts that do consider this text tend to examine biographical tensions, to trace Faulkner's textual sources, or to draw parallels between it and his next fictional effort, *The Sound and the Fury*.[7] This "pastiche" begins in a chapel shortly before dawn on the day that Galwyn becomes a knight. We learn only later that this scene marks the beginning of a reincarnation of sorts; Galwyn has chosen to re-live a portion of life; as Michael Salda notes, Faulkner blurs reality with Galwyn's vision "time and time again in an almost dizzying fashion" so that neither Galwyn nor the reader can distinguish dream from reality (365). Whether "real" or not, Galwyn's experience begins with a teasing vision of his ideal woman in a "dark hurrying stream" (MAY 48), a "face all young and red and white" with "long shining hair like a column of fair sunny water" who reminds Galwyn of "young hyacinths in the spring, and honey and sunlight" (50). He and his constant companions, Pain and Hunger, then embark on a quest for the woman that takes them through an enchanted forest where Galwyn happens upon three princesses, each of whom he seduces and quickly abandons. After seducing the first princess, Yseult (and, incidentally, killing Tristram), Galwyn concludes, "it is not the thing itself that man wants, so much as the wanting of it" (71). He finds no more satisfaction with the other two princesses, Elys and Aelia, so Hunger offers to introduce him to another woman, Hunger's sister, whom he guarantees "will smoothe that look of hunger from your [Galwyn's] face" (81).

Rather than this woman, though, Hunger introduces Galwyn to the Lord of Sleep who promptly asks Galwyn to choose between reliving another phase of life (but not his own) and submersion beneath the waters that he gazed into as the story began. If Galwyn chooses the first option, his future will include more pointless adventures in this continuing cycle, although he cannot return as himself because apparently, as Salda suggests, "Only those whose lives have been 'washed clean' are available for habitation" (363). Submersion beneath those cleansing waters would leave Galwyn's memory "as a smooth surface after rain." He will remember "nothing at all" and will exist beyond the reach of corporeal needs such as Hunger and Pain; moreover, he will attain "Fame" (MAY 84).

Understandably, neither a return to the delusional cycle of someone else's dreams nor the nothingness of submersion appeals to Galwyn. As he gazes into the waters contemplating his decision, he sees the ideal woman he has sought in vain, later identified as "Little sister Death." Galwyn chooses death and goes to her as "one sinking from a fever into a soft and bottomless sleep" (MAY 87). Salda points out, though, that Faulkner's "metacommentarial running heads" call into question the certainty of Galwyn's choice (365). Even as Galwyn chooses suicide, the headings state that he "MEETS ONE HE HAD SEEN IN HIS DREAM AND / HE ENTERS HIS DREAM AGAIN" (86-87). Salda determines that the "choice to die while dreaming is not a choice to die. It is *all* a vision, from first to last, and we have been gazing into Galwyn's dream." Fate's "final cruel joke" appears in Faulkner's own illustrations on the manuscript's endpaper; regardless of "Sleep's promise, the shadow of Galwyn stands behind his tombstone flanked still by the inescapable shadows of Hunger and Pain" (365). The narrator's observation that as Galwyn enters the water "it seemed to him [Galwyn] that he knelt in a dark room waiting for day" also supports such an interpretation (*MAY* 87), because with those words Faulkner returns to exactly the point where *Mayday* began, thus beginning the cycle anew.

While most critics have either neglected *Mayday* or found it a mildly interesting piece of apprentice work, it deserves critical attention, if for no other reason than that it foreshadows themes and character types that Faulkner will continue to work with throughout his career, even into the Snopes trilogy. The work shares particularly close thematic and structural connections with *The Town*, the novel often regarded as the weakest in the trilogy. Cleanth Brooks remarked in 1963 that *The Town* "will seem to some readers a rather frail and limber board placed across two firmly based stools," and elaborated, "In thus avoiding the central novel of the trilogy, one would lose nothing very essential, though he would forgo some incidental comedy that is interesting on its own account" (*William Faulkner* 216). Brooks perhaps overstates the point, but some readers do experience what Woodrow Stroble describes as a "sense of expectations disappointed" after reading the trilogy's middle volume (196). This disappointment stems, at least in part, from *The Town*'s limited style of narration. The other books of the trilogy combine techniques of first person and omniscient narration to lend a somewhat more solid (though still tenuous) sense of the novel's events. In *The Town*, readers must rely solely on the perceptions of three narrators: V.K. Ratliff, the folksy traveling sewing machine agent, observer of human behavior, and by far the most astute of the three narrators; Chick Mallison, the self-proclaimed "voice of Jefferson" who never even witnesses many of the stories that he narrates; and his uncle, Stevens, the ostensibly good-hearted yet less-than-perceptive attorney for Yoknapatawpha County.

This first person narration lends an attractive sense of immediacy and creates the characteristic Faulknerian ambiguity about what exactly happens in *The Town*, although the basic plot seems clear enough. The novel describes Flem Snopes's rise to prominence in Jefferson despite Stevens's quest against "Snopesism." Faulkner gradually reveals the various levels of Flem's plan and shows how Flem eliminates those who stand in the way of his assimilation into Jefferson's upper echelons as president of one of the town's two banks.

Indeed, this prolonged buildup could also motivate the initial widespread dissatisfaction with the second volume; essentially, readers spend most of the novel anticipating Flem's activities. Ratliff compares Flem's feigned ignorance of his wife's affair with Jefferson's mayor, the hidden knowledge that his plan ultimately turns on, to "that twenty-dollar gold piece pinned to your undershirt on your first maiden trip to what you hope is going to be a Memphis whorehouse," and readers, like the narrators, spend most of the novel waiting for Flem, as Ratliff puts it, to "unpin it" (*T* 26). When Flem does effectively "unpin it" by threatening to reveal the affair, the shock of Eula's ensuing suicide and Manfred de Spain's hasty exit from Jefferson hardly makes for a satisfying ending.

Of these limited viewpoints, Stevens's seems, by far, the most restricted. Joseph R. Urgo suggests that by the time of *The Mansion*, Stevens has begun to realize "late in his life, that for all his hypothesizing on good and evil and on justice and injustice . . . no purely good or purely evil actions" exist (*Apocrypha* 200). In *The Town*, however, Stevens still believes that the world has a strict moral framework; he thinks that good and evil exist independently of each other and fancies himself a knight seeking justice and equipped to distinguish between the two. Stevens genuinely seems to wish to do the right thing, yet he lacks the judgment and ability needed to take effective action. His idealism reaches so deeply into his character that he often sees the world not as it is, but as he wishes it to be. For instance, when he says that rumors of Eula and de Spain's affair constitute only "lies—gossip," Maggie, Stevens's twin sister who knows him best, pointedly remarks, "You can see things without looking at them, just like you can hear things without listening" (*T* 44). Similarly, Ratliff later tells Chick that even though Ratliff understands that Flem ultimately desires the respectability that becoming president of de Spain's bank would ensure, he cannot tell Stevens because "he [Stevens] wouldn't believe me." Stevens, Ratliff knows, will have to "learn it his—himself, the hard way" (226, 227).

Stevens's willfully innocent mindset limits almost every aspect of his life because it affects how he perceives or, more accurately, misperceives the world around him. Most notably, Stevens perpetually misestimates Flem. Theresa M. Towner speculates that Stevens focuses on "imaginative projections of what Flem might be doing rather than clear descriptions of what he is doing. The truth of what Flem does therefore shocks him every time" ("It Aint Funny" 331). I would add that Stevens fails to focus on Flem's actions because he truly cannot see them. When he speculates as to how, exactly, Flem informed Will Varner of Eula's affair, for example, he refuses to believe that Flem simply left the note for Mrs. Varner to give to her husband. Stevens knows that Flem could have easily accomplished this, but insists that Flem confronted Varner directly until Ratliff proves him wrong with his eyewitness account (*T* 258-59).

As Ratliff points out, Stevens thinks like a lawyer, and "to a lawyer, if it aint complicated it dont matter whether it works or not because if it aint complicated up enough it aint right and so even if it works, you dont believe it" (260). Stevens misestimates Flem because he assumes that Flem would do things the way that he, Stevens, would do them: choose the highly complicated, yet most satisfying course of action and directly confront Varner. Stevens's mindset traps him so fully that, try as he might, he cannot even begin to think like a Snopes, or, for that matter, like anyone else.

Even such brief considerations of these two works of fiction make it clear that both Faulkner's early and late knights suffer from forms of willful ignorance: Galwyn from an oblivion of his own (or so he thinks) choosing and Stevens from a deluded state from which he cannot escape. They, like the hero of *Sir Gawain and the Green Knight* after his adventure in Bertilak's court, fail to understand fully what transpired. The three characters share other traits like excessive verbosity and a heightened concern with their reputations and manners that make it likely that Faulkner fashioned his "knights" after Sir Gawain. As Salda points out, Galwyn is "not the Gawain of *Sir Gawain and the Green Knight* or Malory" yet "Faulkner does have good reasons for choosing Gawain as his model rather than many other possible knights—Gawain is young, untried as the story begins, 'glib,' attracted to and pursued by women, sexually and morally tempted/compromised in the course of the story, easy to anger, rash in his actions, and wiser by the end of the tale" (354).[8] Other resonances between the Gawain poet's work and *Mayday* and *The Town* suggest that Faulkner had *Sir Gawain and the Green Knight* in mind as he constructed these narratives. Gawain's adventure begins when Bertilak, disguised as the Green Knight, challenges Arthur's court to a Christmas game of exchange, one axe blow for another, with Bertilak taking the first blow. In the face of his court's silence, Arthur feels compelled to accept the challenge, but Gawain quickly takes the contest from him. When Gawain severs the Green Knight's head from his shoulders, the Green Knight retrieves it and says that he will administer his blow in one year at the green chapel. While traveling to meet the Green Knight that next year, Gawain takes shelter in Bertilak's castle and engages in another game of exchange, one in which each man gives the other whatever fortune that day brought. Bertilak tricks Gawain by having his own wife attempt to seduce the young knight; Gawain mostly resists her charms, but accepts her gift of a green girdle that will supposedly protect him from harm during his upcoming encounter. Gawain goes on to meet the Green Knight (Bertilak), and when Bertilak drops the disguise, he mildly rebukes Gawain for concealing the gift. When Bertilak finally reveals that Arthur's sister, Morgan le Fay, engineered the entire episode, Gawain returns to Camelot.

Similarities among these three quests strikingly turn on manipulation; for example, the various narrators relate all three tales at some sort of remove. *Sir Gawain and the Green Knight* begins as the narrator promises to "tell it at once as in town I have heard / it told" (1.2.12-13); *Mayday* begins with the words "And the tale tells" (47); and *The Town* begins with Chick's admission that when the story he narrates began he "wasn't born yet so it was Cousin Gowan who was there and big enough to see and remember and tell me afterward when I was big enough for it to make sense" (3). A single individual also controls the events of all three narratives (Morgan le Fay, Flem, and St. Francis), and they depend upon the complicity of the other characters—especially the guides (Bertilak, Ratliff, Hunger and Pain), who always know more about the meaning of crucial events than do the knights. These guides attempt to lead their knights to knowledge through experience, but all three heroes consistently fail to interpret the many clues as to what actually occurs despite such careful instruction.

A list of such similarities could continue, but Faulkner's deliberate deviations from and inversions of the Green Knight tale present far more interesting possibilities. After noting the similarities between Galwyn and Gawain, Salda reiterates, "all these things do not make Galwyn and Gawain identical. In fact, the contrary is true: Galwyn is *not* Gawain, a point that Faulkner will take some trouble to demonstrate in *Mayday*" (354). Most obviously, Faulkner reworks the three scenes in which Bertilak's wife, the Lady of Hautdesert, tests Gawain's chastity. *Mayday* alters this set of scenes drastically; Galwyn meets with three different women and has no qualms about seducing them. Essentially, he reacts much as the later Gawain, the renowned ladies' man, probably would have, such as when he betrays Sir Pelleas by sleeping with his mistress, Lady Ettard (Malory 138). Like Gawain with Bertilak's wife, Galwyn becomes instantly enthralled when he first glimpses each of the three princesses, and just as Gawain thinks Bertilak's wife "more lovely than Guinevere" (*Sir Gawain* 2.39.18), Galwyn reflects when he first spies Yseult, "all his life before this moment was a stale thing" (MAY 66). In contrast to Gawain's timidity, though, Galwyn takes a much bolder approach and eliminates his opponent by killing Tristram. Whereas Gawain feigns sleep and attempts to avoid the lady's advances by enquiring what "she wishes" (*Sir Gawain* 3.48.22), Galwyn uses words as tools of seduction when he utters his standard line and compares Yseult to "honey and sunlight and young hyacinths"; her beauty has, he says, "robbed him of peace and contentment as a gale strips the leaves from a tree" (MAY 67). His speech "wove such a magic that the Princess Yseult purred like a kitten" (68), and she thinks him a "nice-spoken young man"; her words, however, almost instantly put him off. She begins her chattering diatribe by asking Galwyn, "Do you really think I am beautiful?" The scene quickly and humorously degenerates to a discussion about her hair (67-68). After the two "sojourned in the shade of a tree," Galwyn realizes "that young hyacinths were no longer fresh, once you had picked them" (68). He then convinces Yseult to "put something on" other than "the green veils of this twilight" in order to ward off a "spring cold" and he steals away, reflecting that he "preferred seeing her back to her front, naked or otherwise" (69-70). After escaping, he remarks to Hunger: "It occurs to me . . . that it is not the thing itself that man wants, so much as the wanting of it" (71).

Galwyn's next two encounters play out in much the same fashion. He meets Princess Elys, Faulkner's feminine incarnation of the evening star, presumably seduces her, and sneaks off yet again, this time as she sleeps: "young Sir Galwyn waked and raised himself to his elbow. The Princess Elys yet slept and young Sir Galwyn looked upon her in a vague sadness, and he kissed her sleeping mouth with a feeling of pity for her and of no particular pride in himself, and he rose quietly and passed without the tent" (MAY 72). As Galwyn leaves Elys, he meets Princess Aelia, an even more impressive incarnation of the morning star. She sweeps him into her golden chariot driven by nine white dolphins, and he initially thinks her the woman from his dream. When they first kiss while plummeting toward the earth, the narrator observes of Galwyn, "Never had his heart known such ecstasy! he was a god and a falling star, consuming the whole world in a single long swooping rush through measureless regions of horror and delight down down, leaving behind him no change of light nor any sound" (78-79). Yet after this experience, he nevertheless awakens alone in the forest with a sigh of relief. Hunger observes his dissatisfaction and remarks: "Ay, Sir Galwyn, and yet and yet. You have known the bride of a king before ever her husband looked upon her, you have possessed, in the persons of the daughters of the two most important minor princes in Christendom, the morning and the evening stars, and yet you have gained nothing save a hunger which gives you no ease" (79-80). Hunger then observes, "Man is a buzzing fly beneath the inverted glass tumbler of his illusions" (80).

In contrast to Galwyn, Stevens reacts during his three meetings with Eula much as the younger Gawain of the Green Knight tale does when the Lady of Hautdesert visits his chamber.[9] Stevens's first glimpse of Eula enchants him, but, as Ratliff remarks in *The Mansion*, "when Eula Varner taken that first one look of hern at Lawyer—or let him take that first one look of hisn at her, whichever way you want to put it" it was like "when you finally see the woman that had ought to been yourn all the time, only it's already too late" because she "is already married to somebody else." Ratliff also acknowledges a sense of possibility similar to that pervading the scene between Gawain and the lady and adds, "Except it wasn't too late. It aint never too late and wont never be" (434). But, Ratliff adds, "Lawyer didn't know all that yet neither" (435). Like the lady's pursuit of Gawain, Eula's attention takes Stevens totally by surprise; when she sends the note requesting that he wait for her in his office that evening, Stevens "didn't even know who it was from" after reading it (*T* 78). And just as the lady steals into Gawain's room and "quickly" catches him (*Sir Gawain* 3.49.3), Faulkner also utilizes the metaphor of the hunt in his initial scene between Eula and Stevens (Harley 111). Indeed, Stevens thinks before Eula even arrives that he "would probably bolt, flee, run home to Maggie" (*T* 79), and he takes care to leave the door open, despite the cold, to preserve the opportunity for such an escape.

Stevens barely manages to survive the encounter without physically fleeing after Eula arrives and offers herself to him as boldly as does Bertilak's wife. The lady tells Gawain, "To my body will you welcome be / of delight to take your fill; / for need constraineth me / to serve you, and I will" (*Sir Gawain* 3.49.30-33); Eula far less poetically proposes that she and Stevens "Do it here. In your office," and her offer terrifies Stevens as much as the lady's does Gawain. Stevens repeatedly questions "'Here?' . . . like a parrot" (*T* 81), and later exclaims "Dont touch me" when he feels trapped by her request that he simply shut "the door before it gets so cold" (82). Stevens, given his analytical nature, tries to ascertain her motives, whereas Gawain never thinks to ask what motivates Bertilak's wife. Stevens speculates that Eula came to him because either Flem or de Spain sent her, and she admits, "Maybe I did. . . . Maybe at first." An earlier question, though, hints at another reason Eula might pursue Stevens. When he rebuffs her, she asks, "You mean you dont want to? . . . I thought that was what you wanted," and then wonders, "What did you do it for?" (82). The "it" could refer either to Stevens's challenging de Spain at the Christmas ball or the lawsuit that he files against him on behalf of the city, but they both amount to pathetically ineffective attempts to defend Eula's honor.

Eula's behavior stymies critics almost as much as it does Stevens, and they have read her actions in a variety of ways. In the type of interpretation that remained standard for decades, Brooks noted as early as 1963 that Eula's offer "is so direct as to seem brutal" (*William Faulkner* 196). Dawn Trouard, however, evaluates this scene in light of Eula's limited options given the novel's patriarchal culture and believes that she is "debilitated and frustrated." Trouard suggests that Eula's "emotional reserves" allow her to offer herself to Stevens "*practically*, despite sanctions—including Gavin's—prohibiting her exercise of freedom and power" (289). While Faulkner gives us too little to know Eula's motivations or mindset definitively, this deviation from the Gawain story may imply that regardless of what Stevens believes, Eula visits his office of her own volition and offers to repay his kindness in the best way she knows how. She obviously knows that Stevens finds her desirable, and she offers him what she thinks (and he thinks) he wants. When pressed, Eula says that she came to Stevens because she thought him "unhappy," and she does not "like unhappy people. They're a nuisance. Especially when it can—" At that point, Stevens cuts her off and launches into a righteous rejection of the "pity" that he thinks she offers. His tirade, though, only gives voice to his interpretation of her offer, one Eula neither confirms nor denies; for all he knows, she might have completed her thought with something to the effect of "especially when it can be so wonderful for both of us." When Stevens finally stops talking, Eula implies that he has it all wrong when she says, "Dont expect. You just are, and you need, and you must, and so you do. That's all. Dont waste time expecting." She then offers another possible reason for her visit: "Maybe it's because you're a gentleman and I never knew one before" (*T* 83). Her comment could mean that Stevens rejects her advances or defends her honor from some gentlemanly impulse, but it could also mean that she came to his office because she thinks him a gentleman and she finds that status attractive. After all, Bertilak's lady tells Gawain in the similar situation:

> if I should exchange at my choice and choose me a husband,
> for the noble nature I know, Sir Knight, in thee here,
> in beauty and bounty and bearing so gay—
> of which earlier I have heard, and hold it now true—
> then no lord alive would I elect before you. (*Sir Gawain* 3.51.9-13)

When Eula says that she "never knew" a gentleman before, she admits that although she may sleep with de Spain, she does not think that he belongs to the same social or moral class as Stevens. Her comments, of course, appeal to Stevens's vanity, but perhaps she also seeks from him something her relationship with de Spain lacks; that would certainly make more sense than Stevens's theory (pity), and near the novel's conclusion Faulkner suggests as much. As Stevens and Ratliff return from Eula's graveside, Stevens, desperately trying to figure out what motivated Eula to take her own life, thinks aloud, "She loved, had a capacity to love, for love, to give and accept love. Only she tried twice and failed twice to find somebody not just strong enough to deserve, earn it, match it, *but even brave enough to accept it*" (emphasis added, *Town* 315). Stevens believes that Eula tried to love two men, ostensibly Hoake McCarron and de Spain.[10] While those two lovers may not have deserved, earned, or matched her love, they did at least accept the physical expression of it. Perhaps Eula tried and failed to love three times, the third failure because Stevens lacked the courage to "accept it."[11]

Moreover, Stevens does not believe that Eula genuinely finds him attractive; Brooks speculates that Stevens fails to recognize Eula's comment as a compliment because "evidently Gavin fears that a gentleman is something less than a man, his power and vigor enfeebled by refinement" (*William Faulkner* 212). While I would argue that Stevens simply fears Eula, period, whatever his reasons, he, like Gawain, manages to talk his way out of the situation.[12] The Gawain poet writes, "She was an urgent wooer, / that lady fair of face; / the knight with speeches pure / replied in every case" (3.50.19-22). One of Gawain's many resistance tactics involves pleading inadequacy; as he tells the lady, "I am a knight unworthy, as well indeed I know" (3.50.4). She, however, will have none of it. She appeals to his vanity and invokes his reputation for courtesy when she remarks that a knight as courteous as Gawain "so long with a lady could hardly have lingered / without craving a kiss" (3.52.10-11). Likewise, Stevens expresses a similar concern for courtesy in Faulkner's parallel scene. After he accuses Eula of attempting to seduce him at Flem's or de Spain's urging, he retracts the allegation, saying, "I didn't mean that," and asks Eula to forgive him (*T* 82). Stevens's concern for courtesy, though, does not permit Eula to touch him. When Stevens all but leaps away from Eula, exclaiming "Dont touch me," she asks, "Why are you afraid?" He then escapes "out of the trap now and even around her" and practically runs for the door (83-84). He fails, however, to answer her question. What, indeed, instills such fear? Stevens indicates a couple of possible reasons, though only in a roundabout way: "You told me not to expect; why dont you try it yourself? We've all bought Snopeses here, whether we wanted to or not; you of all people should certainly know that." Stevens goes on, "But nothing can hurt you if you refuse it, not even a brass-stealing Snopes. And nothing is of value that costs nothing so maybe you will value this refusal at what I value it cost me" (84). Stevens, then, implies that he refuses her in order to circumvent rejection. He believes that a physical relationship would have meant nothing to her, and he rejects her to avoid suffering that devastating realization. Ratliff intuits as much: "there was more folks among the Helens and Juliets and Isoldes and Guineveres than jest the Launcelots and Tristrams and Romeos and Parises." He concludes, "Not ever body had Helen, but then not ever body lost her neither" (89). After the fact, Stevens, of course, thinks of himself as rejecting Eula's advances to maintain his ideal of her in the tradition of courtly love that Brooks articulates, but even Brooks notes that Stevens "only partly understands his motives" during "his encounter with Eula at his office" (*William Faulkner* 199). That Stevens's fears of inadequacy, then, remain firmly behind his ideological framework seems clear when he finishes another of Eula's unarticulated sentences. Eula tells Stevens that de Spain "is enjoying himself" with regard to Stevens's lawsuit "Because you cant. . . ." Stevens then thinks, "Because even she stopped then; even the insentient sea compassionate too but then I could bear that too; I could even say it for her: 'Manfred wouldn't really mind because just I cant hurt him, harm him, do him any harm; not Manfred, not just me, no matter what I do'" (*T* 82-83). Stevens, then, thinks of Manfred as an invincible foe, the metaphorical equivalent of the Green Knight.

Ten years pass before Stevens is alone with Eula again; the second meeting inverts elements of the Gawain story. Bertilak's wife calls on Gawain quite early in order to "wear away" his "will" (*Sir Gawain* 3.58.22). He, however, has prepared for her arrival and "graciously then welcomed her first" when she "passed to the curtain and peeped at the knight" (3.59.1-2). Stevens and the Lady of Hautdesert effectively change places when Faulkner revises this scenario; when Stevens arrives on Eula's doorstep promptly at nine, ready to plead his case for why Eula should allow Linda to leave Jefferson and go away to college, Eula "was prepared, self house and soul too" (*T* 193). By repositioning Eula, Faulkner emphasizes how restrained, or perhaps contained, Eula has become during the ten years following Stevens's rejection. Flem has, to his way of thinking, turned her into an accessory, the living, breathing equivalent of his bow tie. Moreover, she knows how little power she holds, as becomes clear when Stevens describes the furniture-shopping expedition in relation to Flem's becoming vice president of de Spain's bank: "To be exactly what he needed to exactly fit exactly what he was going to be tomorrow after it was announced: a vice president's wife and child along with the rest of the vice president's furniture in the vice president's house? Is that what you tried to tell me?" Eula more or less agrees: "Something like that" (197). She similarly has no control over Linda's future and tells Stevens, "It's not me that wont let her go away" (196).

Linda's fate highlights the second way that Faulkner inverts this scene from its counterpart in *Sir Gawain and the Green Knight*. During her second visit, Bertilak's wife proposes that Gawain tutor her in the ways of love:

> Surely, you that are so accomplished and so courtly in your vows
> should be prompt to expound to a young pupil
> by signs and examples the science of lovers.
> Why? Are you ignorant who all honour enjoy?
> Or else you esteem me too stupid to understand your courtship? (*Sir Gawain* 3.60.18-22).

Gawain replies that he can teach her nothing because she possesses "far more skill / in that art by the half than a hundred of such / as I am, or shall ever be while on earth I remain, / it would be folly manifold, in faith, my lady!" (3.61.8-11). In *The Mansion*, Ratliff sincerely thinks of Eula in similar fashion when he reflects that she "never needed to be educated nowhere because jest what the Lord had already give her by letting her stand up and breathe and maybe walk around a little now and then was trouble and danger enough for ever male man in range" (435). When Stevens meets her again, he implies that he holds the same opinion and doubts that Eula "was ever in her life unready for anything that just wore pants" (*T* 193). Eula seeks an education not for herself, though, but for her daughter. By this time, Stevens has already transferred a portion of his devotion to Linda and has spent several years "forming her mind" as he first did with Melisandre Backus years before (*T* 158). In light of Stevens's attentions, Eula's suggestion that he marry Linda is not unreasonable, as Stevens thinks. For example, in *The Mansion*, several characters think marriage a viable option for Stevens and Linda. Ratliff even asks Stevens, "Why didn't you marry her?" When Stevens replies, "Because she wasn't but nineteen," Ratliff retorts, "And you are all of thirty-five, aint you" (467). Later, Chick recalls Ratliff's telling him of Stevens's prediction that Linda's "doom would be to love once and lose him and then to mourn" and says that Stevens refuses to marry her because "he had his own prognosis to defend, make his own words good no matter who anguished and suffered" (528). Chick also points out to Stevens, "Mother says she's [Linda's] been in love with you all her life, only she was too young to know it and you were too much of a gentleman to tell her" (505). Marriage would allow Linda to get out from under Flem's thumb and would free Eula to do the same. Stevens, though, either cannot or will not see the obvious. He exclaims, "Dont you see, that's what I'm after: to set her free of Jefferson, not tie her down to it still more, still further, still worse, but to set her free?" Eula, immediately sensing the true source of Stevens's reservation, tries to convince him that "marriage is the only fact. The rest of it is still the poet's romantic dream. Marry her. She'll have you. Right now, in the middle of all this, she wont know how to say No. Marry her." Stevens replies only, "Goodbye" (*T* 199).

During her final meeting with him, Eula continues trying to convince Stevens to give up his romantic notions and offer his practical assistance. This meeting, like the corresponding one in the Gawain story, features "great peril" between the lady and her knight (*Sir Gawain* 3.70.19). The Lady of Hautdesert arrives in Gawain's chamber and "pressed him so closely, / led him so near the line, that at last he must needs / either refuse her with offence or her favours there take" (3.71.1-3). She even says, "Now shame you deserve, / if you love not one that lies alone here beside you" (3.71.10-11). Gawain, of course, refuses her, declaring, "Nay! lover have I none, / and none will have meanwhile" (3.71.21-22). By rejecting her, he chooses the option that he thinks presents the lesser of two evils—he declines to betray Bertilak and accepts the cost of offending his wife with discourtesy. Gawain does not emerge totally unscathed, though. The wife attempts to give him two gifts, the first a costly ring, which he refuses (3.73.1), and then the green girdle that prevents its wearer from being "killed by any cunning of hand" (3.74.9). The protection the girdle could supposedly provide during his impending encounter with the Green Knight proves too strong a temptation for Gawain and he accepts the gift, agreeing to the lady's request that he break his covenant with Bertilak by concealing it (3.74.16-20).

Similarly, Eula initiates her final meeting with Stevens when she has Chick deliver the note to him that reads, "*Please meet me at your office at ten tonight*" (T 274). Stevens instinctively realizes that this meeting will involve another test and wonders, "*What more can you want of me than I have already failed to do?*" (275). A few pages later, he seems to view the impending meeting as a final chance to reject rather than to save Eula, and he thinks of it as "the one last chance to choose, decide: whether or not to say *Why me? Why bother me? Why cant you let me alone?*" (279). He, of course, says nothing of the sort when Eula enters his office. He notes that Eula has "been to the beauty shop," and she replies, "That's where I met Chick." Stevens goes on with characteristic loquaciousness, "'But not inside,' I said, already trying to stop. 'Not where water and soap are coeval, conjunctive,' still trying to stop. 'Not for a few years yet,' and did." He then gets right to the point and asks Eula, "Tell me. What was it he [Flem] took out there to your mother yesterday that had old Will on the road to town at two oclock this morning?" Stevens apparently misinterprets Eula's actions once again; unwilling to confront the events of the previous night in such a direct manner, she evades his question by remarking, "There's your cob pipe. . . . You've got three of them. I've never seen you smoke one. When do you smoke them?" (281). Stevens's avoidance is not characteristic. In *Intruder in the Dust*, Stevens speaks "through" the smoke from his pipe to suggest that he "is blowing smoke" with his explanations concerning "the South's position on the Negro question" (Polk, "Crime Fiction" 8). As Polk concludes in *Children of the Dark House*, "It could hardly be clearer that in *Intruder* Gavin Stevens is largely blowing smoke—not altogether because of what he says but rather because of the relationship between what he says and what he actually does" (222). The obvious phallic implications of the perennially unlit pipe in *The Town* aside, Stevens ironically refuses to blow smoke, figuratively or literally, on the one occasion when Eula desires such distraction. Instead, he again questions her about the previous night's events. She then mentions the will and begins to tell him the specifics of how Flem "beat" Linda by using her filial affection to gain control of her inheritance. Linda, however, "didn't even know there had been a battle and she had surrendered" (285); Eula says that Linda "believes she thought of it, wanted to do it, did it, herself. Nobody can tell her otherwise" (282).

Eula hints that Stevens's influence over Linda could potentially match Flem's when she says that the conflict erupted over the "school business. When you [Stevens] told her she wanted to go, get away from here" (T 282). As Eula talks, she keeps reminding Stevens of Flem's sway over Linda, that he "was her father, you see. You've got to remember that. Can you?" (284). Stevens, though, shifts the conversation back to Eula's responsibility and points out that if Eula and de Spain leave, Linda "is lost," whatever action Eula takes: "Either to go with you, if that were possible, while you desert her father for another man; or stay here in all the stink without you to protect her from it and learn at last that he is not her father at all and so she has nobody, nobody" (289-90). Eula repeats her request again and offers Stevens a metaphorical ring when she implores him to marry Linda. He, like Gawain, flatly refuses her offer and suggests that Eula turn to de Spain for help. She, of course, has already tried that (290); Stevens truly represents her last hope, so she tries again. Using his given name for the first time, she pleads, "Marry her, Gavin," but Stevens only caustically paraphrases his interpretation of her reasoning and says, "Change her name by marriage, then she wont miss the one she will lose when you abandon her" (291). Eula persists, though, and he finally agrees to marry Linda only "if or when I become convinced that conditions are going to become such that something will have to be done, and nothing else but marrying me can help her, and she will have me. But have me, take me. Not just give up, surrender" (292).

Eula recognizes this offer as the best she will likely get and makes Stevens "swear" to marry Linda in that event, "even if she wont have you. Even after that. Even if she w—you cant marry her" (*T* 292). Eula surely realizes that Stevens's promise undoes itself, that he "cant" offer any real, practical assistance by marrying Linda because he cannot give up what she earlier referred to as "the poet's romantic dream" of ideal love (199). Stevens tells Eula that he wants Linda to choose him, not just "give up, surrender" to marriage and a safe life in Jefferson (292), but in *The Mansion*, we learn that he also refuses marriage because agreeing would mean abandoning his dream of Eula. Stevens has likely spoken to Ratliff about this last meeting; even though Ratliff claims to "presume on a little more than jest evidence" (M 456), he does so with accuracy and mentions many specific details of this final meeting.[13] While Ratliff could have learned of the meeting from Eula, he later says in *The Mansion* that Stevens "finally told me what little he actively knowed" but "it was jest evidence I had already presumed on" (458). From all he hears, Ratliff surmises that when Eula asked Stevens to marry Linda, "it was like she had said right out in public that he wouldn't a had no hope [of having a relationship with Eula] even if Manfred de Spain hadn't never laid eyes on her." Stevens reacts as he does because "if he could jest get that 'No' out quick enough, it would be like maybe she hadn't actively said what she said, and he would still not be destroyed" (M 457). Thus Stevens inadvertently dooms the woman he most loves because he cannot abandon his romantic dream of her. Perhaps, like young John Sartoris in this chapter's epigraph from *Flags in the Dust*, Stevens does not wait "for Time and its furniture to teach him that the end of wisdom is to dream high enough not to lose the dream in the seeking of it" (597). Given Stevens's age and disposition, though, it seems more likely that he is incapable of learning such a lesson. Faulkner further emphasizes Stevens's misplaced priorities when he insists on driving Eula home, saying, "A lady, walking home alone at—it's after midnight. What will Otis Harker [the night marshal] say? You see, I've got to be a man too; I cant face Otis Harker otherwise since you wont stop being a lady to him until after tomorrow's south-bound train" (*T* 292). Rather than taking the one action that could save both Eula and Linda, Stevens bumbles along with his misplaced gestures of courtesy and romantic notions, safely insulated from reality for the time being. In a 1955 interview with Cynthia Grenier, Faulkner spoke to the value of the brand of direct action that Stevens avoids. Grenier asked Faulkner about his favorites among his own characters and he turned the question back on her, asking "who are *your* favorite characters?" She said that she admired Isaac McCaslin because "he underwent the baptism in the forest, because he rejected his inheritance." Faulkner questioned further, "And do you think it's a good thing for a man to reject an inheritance?" She replied, "Yes," and asked Faulkner, "You don't think it's a good thing for him to have done so?" Faulkner said, "Well, I think a man ought to do more than just repudiate. He should have been more affirmative instead of shunning people." Grenier asked, "Do you think that any of your characters succeed in being more affirmative?" Faulkner, perhaps still thinking of inaction, replied, "Yes, I do. There was Gavin Stevens. He was a good man but he didn't succeed in living up to his ideal" (*LG* 224-25).

Faulkner also complicates the Gawain story in quite interesting ways as it relates to the outcomes of the tests that his characters face. Wendy Clein points out that Gawain fails Bertilak's final test because his "instinctual fear of death rises to the surface, leading to his violation of chivalric rules" (101). In *Mayday*, Galwyn, though, chooses death and goes to it willingly. Philip Cohen posits that Galwyn, "disillusioned," finally "commits suicide by drowning himself in a river in which he sees the face from the vision" rather than accept the fatalistic view of his existence that Hunger and Pain describe ("Faulkner's Player" 18), one in which he "is but a handful of damp clay" that his two companions "draw hither and yon at will until the moisture is gone completely out of him" (*MAY* 57-58). I would argue that, instead of suffering from disillusionment, Galwyn chooses suicide because he has become free from illusion. This is not to say that Galwyn's freedom equals nothingness; Galwyn remains open to the possibility of the creation of meaning in a way that the idealistic Stevens can never accept, as he finally recognizes the pointlessness of his efforts and wonders "if his restless seeking through the world had been only a devious unnecessary way of returning to a place he need never have left" (*MAY* 82). He also realizes the damage he has done to others as he gazes into the river and the "glittering wreckage" of the women he has wronged passes before his eyes (86). Salda, to be sure, points out that Galwyn's decision offers only the illusion of choice, but Galwyn nevertheless thinks that he makes it

(362-65). As such he, along with the likes of Quentin Compson, becomes one of the early Faulknerian tragic heroes who, when faced with the choice between grief and nothing, chooses nothing.

With their unillusioned (or perhaps only less illusioned) choices, Galwyn and Gawain seem very much Stevens's opposites. This difference becomes apparent as Faulkner moves into the final section of *The Town*, and Stevens, along with the rest of Jefferson, waits for a very different kind of axe stroke from the one Gawain anticipates. Chick compares the community's awareness and passive acceptance of Eula and de Spain's affair to a "barked over" nail driven into a tree. The entire town continues to expect Flem finally to acknowledge the affair and force them to do the same. As Chick puts it, they continue to do so "until one day the saw or the axe goes into it [the tree] and hits that old nail" (T 266). He elaborates:

> As far as Jefferson was concerned it had already touched it; we were merely waiting now to see in what direction the fragments of that particular tree in our wood (not the saw itself, never the saw: if that righteous and invincible moral blade flew to pieces at the contact, let us all dissolute too since the very fabric of Baptist and Methodist life were delusion, nothing) would scatter and disintegrate. (270)

That moment, though, never comes; Eula's suicide neatly circumvents it. Faulkner nevertheless connects Stevens's role in Eula's suicide to Gawain's experience with the Green Knight through a variety of details. The night before Gawain has vowed to meet the Green Knight, he sleeps little and "at the crow of every cock he recalls well his tryst" (*Sir Gawain* 4.80.11). Similarly, after Stevens leaves Eula, he returns home and spends the night listening to "the damned mocking bird" that "for three nights now" has made "his constant racket in Maggie's pink dogwood just under my bedroom window" (T 293). Stevens thinks that the "trick" to not hearing the bird would "be to divide, not him but his racket, the having to listen to him" by splitting into "one Gavin Stevens to cross his dark gallery too and into the house and up the stairs to cover his head in the bedclothes, losing in his turn a dimension [presumably the other, or second incarnation] of Gavin Stevens, an ectoplasm of Gavin Stevens impervious to cold and hearing too to bear its half of both, bear its half or all of any other burdens anyone wanted to shed and shuck" (293-94). His uneasy meditation has less to do with the mockingbird than with his discomfort over assuming the burden of "a young abandoned girl's responsibility" (294), and the longing to divide himself into separate physical and spiritual dimensions recalls Gawain's struggle between the physical temptation presented by the Lady of Hautdesert and his moral desire not to betray Bertilak on the eve of his conflict with the Green Knight.

Stevens never reaches such a moment of decision, though, because Eula kills herself instead of running away with de Spain. Early in *The Town*, Maggie says of her brother's adulation of Eula, "You dont marry Semiramis: you just commit some form of suicide for her" (44). The "form" of that suicide emerges quite unexpectedly when Stevens fails Eula's final test. Gawain's acceptance of the green girdle leads only to his own minor injury, a nick as punishment from Bertilak for lacking "loyalty" (*Sir Gawain* 4.95.9); Galwyn's choice injures (perhaps) only himself; but Stevens's failure to act beyond his frail excuse for a promise to marry Linda leads to Eula's suicide, a likelihood many scholars have alluded to. For example, John Lewis Longley speculates that Stevens's "refusal to promise to marry Linda may have brought on Eula's decision to save Linda from Flem in the only way she can, by killing herself, to leave Linda 'a mere suicide for a mother instead of a whore'" (45).[14] Whatever her reasons, Eula likely did not plan to kill herself before meeting Stevens, although she probably entertained the idea as a last resort. When she met Chick and passed on the note summoning Stevens, Chick noticed that "she really did look both ways along the street before she turned and started toward me" (*T* 271-72). With Chick's observation, Faulkner calls attention to a level of caution uncharacteristic of a suicidal person. Of course, Eula could want to sacrifice herself in suicide to accomplish goals for herself and her daughter that an accidental death would not have achieved. Holli G. Levitsky points to some of these potential goals in her reading of Eula's suicide as an act that "textually repeated and thematically regenerated by her love for her daughter and generating a new life for her daughter, confirms her subjectivity" (38). But by focusing on Eula's cautionary glance up and down the street, Faulkner at least highlights her desire to live, the strength of her instinct for self-preservation.

Even though Stevens fails Eula, Chick believes that he emerges in the eyes of the town as "the pure one, the only pure one," in contrast to de Spain and Flem. De Spain leaves town in disgrace, and the town condemns Flem for not taking more decisive action, such as blowing "them both, his wife and her fancy banker both, clean out of Jefferson" (*T* 300). Chick says that because all of Jefferson knew that Stevens desired Eula but "hadn't been Mrs Snopes's lover too," the townspeople recognize him as "the bereaved, the betrayed husband forgiving for the sake of the half-orphan child" (300). Whether or not Chick's assessment is accurate, the ever-dramatic Stevens accepts it and even thinks himself the only one qualified to lead Eula's funeral service (301).[15] Faulkner almost certainly uses this odd desire to signify that Stevens imagines himself purified after the fashion of Launcelot, who "did all the observance of the service himself" while burying Guinevere (Malory 933). Maggie points out the inappropriateness of Stevens's proposition when, in exasperation, she exclaims, "Gavin, at first I thought I would never understand why Eula did it. But now I'm beginning to believe that maybe I do. Do you want Linda to have to say afterward that another bachelor had to bury her?" (*T* 301).

Stevens does not conduct the service, but he plays a much more pivotal role in creating Eula's "monument." As Ratliff says, he "helped Linda hunt through that house and her mother's things until they found the right photograph and had it—Lawyer still—enlarged, the face part, and sent it to Italy to be carved into a . . . yes, medallion to fasten onto the front of the monument" (*T* 306). Ratliff remains adamant that the monument belongs and pays tribute to Flem, as it most certainly does; Flem "paid for it, first thought of it, planned and designed it, picked out what size and what was to be wrote on it—the face and the letters" (307). As Trouard notes, Eula's epitaph memorializes "the dark irony of Flem's utter triumph": "In the discourse of the fathers, inscribed on materials that are intended to last, homage is paid to the qualities that benefit the deceased wife of the new president of the bank. The monument is to Flem" (284). Flem accordingly chooses an epitaph that, in death, forces Eula to occupy the position that she declined in life:

> EULA VARNER SNOPES
> 1889   1927
> A virtuous Wife is a Crown to her Husband
> Her Children rise and call Her Blessed (*T* 312)

Or, as Trouard puts it, "Eula, much like 'My Last Duchess,' is frozen in and by male discourse" (284). Linda may well rise and call her mother blessed in *The Mansion*, but Eula never played the role of "virtuous Wife," at least in the traditional sense that Flem wants to superimpose upon her. Ratliff continues:

> that marble medallion face that Lawyer had picked out and selected . . . never looked like Eula a-tall you thought at first, never looked like nobody nowhere you thought at first, until you were wrong because it never looked like all women because what it looked like was one woman that ever man that was lucky enough to have been a man would say, "Yes, that's her. I knowed her five years ago or ten years ago or fifty years ago and you would a thought that by now I would a earned the right not to have to remember her anymore. . . ." (*T* 311-12)

In *The Mansion*, Ratliff similarly describes the medallion as "the same face that ever young man no matter how old he got would still never give up hope and belief that some day before he died he would finally be worthy to be wrecked and ruined and maybe even destroyed by it" (465). Ratliff's description makes clear that, in death, Stevens has finally managed to force Eula into the role of goddess that she refused in life.[16] As Brooks first pointed out, Stevens never sees the real Eula:

> Gavin is determined to regard Eula as a kind of Mississippi Madame Bovary. But Eula, healthy, earthy, and strong-minded, is the least romantic person in town. The numinous haze that she wears, the special aura that witnesses to her divinity, resides in the eye of the beholder. Throughout her life she confounds Gavin by not behaving

as he expects the heroine of a romantic novel to behave: she is dispassionate and practical. And at the end, she confounds him once more by killing herself: the dispassionate woman is capable of the heroic act, though Gavin persists in interpreting her act in terms of his romantic dream. (*William Faulkner* 217)

Eula's monument, then, pays tribute to Stevens's unawareness at least as much as it does to the construct of Flem's respectability.[17]

On reflection, the gulf that separates Galwyn from Stevens seems quite wide. Galwyn is a figure characteristic of Faulkner's early, nihilistic heroes, an untried knight who, as he gradually gains experience and loses illusions concerning the meaning of life, comes to choose the oblivion of death over the pointless repetition of a meaningless existence. In *The Town*, though, because Stevens retains the very illusions that Galwyn loses, he causes far more destruction than does Galwyn. Just before the conclusion of *Mayday*, the Lord of Sleep tells Galwyn, "Man should beware of Experience as he should beware of all women, for with her or without her he will be miserable, but without her he will not be dangerous" (85). It would seem that the Lord of Sleep is wrong, at least as far as Stevens is concerned; he remains in his illusioned fog even as *The Town* concludes, and, though his intentions seem pure enough, the results seem questionable indeed.

Part of this character evolution likely stems from the political climate of Faulkner's world as he composed *The Town*.[18] He began writing the novel during the late stages of his most politically active period, and he seemed to view it as an escape from public life; he wrote to Saxe Commins as he began *The Town*, "Miss. such an unhappy state to live in now, that I need something like a book to get lost in" (*SL* 390).[19] He finished the novel in September 1956, and Random House published it in May 1957. Faulkner gradually decreased his political involvement as he became engaged with composition and effectively curtailed this active political interlude when he wrote to Frederick A. Colwell in May 1958, declining to travel to Russia on a state department mission: "I am 60 now and have possibly done all the good work I am capable of, was intended to do" (413).

The political ideology that Faulkner espoused during this period remains far too elaborate to address fully here; indeed, Faulkner may not have completely understood it himself, but it clearly operated, as does his fiction, as a series of opposing tensions. Faulkner believed the South responsible for and capable of solving its own problems and deeply feared Northern interference, a second period of Reconstruction that he knew would impress reformation upon the South unless it enacted such changes itself. As he said in Virginia, "Let us say to the North: All right, it is our problem, and we will solve it." Since "he, the Negro, is not yet capable of, or refuses to accept, the responsibilities of equality . . . we, the white man, must take him in hand and teach him that responsibility" (*FU* 210). People typically remember Faulkner best for conservative positions such as this one and for the most notorious of his many conflicted stances, his moderate position on racial reform during the 1950s and 60s that managed only to anger proponents of both sides. Though apparently well-intentioned, the infamous appeal couched in his "Letter to a Northern Editor" asking reformers to "Go slow now" offered little satisfaction at the time and seems, in retrospect, to reflect more than anything else some level of personal ambivalence (*ESPL* 87). Joseph Blotner identifies Faulkner as a "gradualist," and notes, "for a man of his age, time, and place, this represented an advanced position—one which would bring upon him abuse and even threats from his own region, while at the same time provoking criticism from the outsiders who thought he hadn't gone far enough" (*A Biography* [1974] 1252). Towner acknowledges the complexity of Faulkner's position when she guardedly uses the word "conflicted" to describe Faulkner's racial attitudes:

> Calling those beliefs "conflicted" perhaps runs the risk of characterizing them so broadly as to make them incapable of analysis, yet that word is the one that encompasses both Faulkner's wish to protect Autherine Lucy's life from the crowds in Tuscaloosa, Alabama, and his reluctance to invite the half-black, half-Puerto Rican Juano Hernandez to a wrap party at Rowan Oak for the filming of *Intruder in the Dust*. (*Color Line* 119)

Faulkner fared little better when he stepped into the arena of national politics in his post-Nobel years. This foray helped foster an image of "the canonized Faulkner" which, Urgo notes, "is often presented as a sagacious old man with strong humanist moral fiber who believed in God and did not mean to drink so much" (*Apocrypha* 3). Such a persona contrasted starkly with the nihilistic, rebellious Faulkner of the 1930s; as Warren Beck put it in 1961, "the alleged *enfant terrible* of American fiction in the thirties has become the recognized old humanist" (4-5). Such perceptions foster a dualistic view of Faulkner that, for many critics, divides the early fiction from the later. Thus many continue, wrongly, to think of Faulkner as a Southern moderate in racial matters who ventured into the political realm at the expense of that later fiction. As Urgo remarks, "According to the story, the post-Laureate Faulkner suffered a decline in creative power and artistic intensity, the result of which is that 'Faulkner redeemed' was never quite as powerful or convincing as the 'fallen' Faulkner" (*Apocrypha* 5).[20] Or, as long-time friend Phil Stone put it, Faulkner suffered from "Nobelitis in the Head" after receiving the award (Blotner, *A Biography* [1984] 562).[21]

The evolution of Faulkner's Gawain figures, however, suggests that critics such as Carothers, Polk, Towner, Urgo, and others who champion Faulkner's later fiction are correct in that the nihilist had neither reformed nor fallen victim to the perils of didactic fiction, even as late as the composition of *The Town*. Stevens, rather than simplistically speaking for Faulkner, instead becomes the perfect vehicle for demonstrating the havoc that a well-meaning, though ill-informed, crusader can wreak. Faulkner's political forays during this period likely taught him much about the dangers of hollow reformers such as Stevens, men unwilling to listen to, or perhaps even incapable of considering, viewpoints that fall outside their own idealistic vision of how the world should operate. In "On Fear: Deep South in Labor: Mississippi," tellingly subtitled "(The American Dream: What Happened to It?)," Faulkner observes:

> In fact, there are people in the South, Southerners born, . . . who love our land—not love white people specifically nor love Negroes specifically, but our land, our country: our climate and geography, the qualities in our people, white and Negro too, for honesty and fairness, the splendors in our traditions, the glories in our past—enough to try to reconcile them, even at the cost of displeasing both sides: the contempt of the Northern radicals who believe we dont do enough, the contumely and threats of our own Southern reactionaries who are convinced that anything we do is already too much. (*ESPL* 95)

This description characterizes Faulkner's own position as he perceived it, and Stevens certainly loves the South in such fashion; however, Stevens cannot sufficiently disengage himself from his beloved Yoknapatawpha to view it at an adequate remove. Faulkner makes Stevens's position clear when, just before he meets with Eula for the final time, he surveys all of the town from "a ridge" beyond "Seminary Hill" (*T* 276), perhaps the same ridge from which Chick's "whole native land" unfolds "beneath him like a map" in *Intruder in the Dust* (398). While that description emphasizes Chick's growing disconnection from the land and the people and how it facilitates a more reasonable view of both, the remarkably similar passage in *The Town* insists upon Stevens's inability to separate himself, as Chick does, from the panorama of "all Yoknapatawpha in the dying last of day," despite his claim of being "detached as God himself for this moment" (277):

> They are all here, supine beneath you, stratified and superposed, osseous and durable with the frail dust and the phantoms:—the rich alluvial river-bottom land of old Issetibbeha, the wild Chickasaw king, with his Negro slaves and his sister's son called Doom who murdered his way to the throne and, legend said (record itself said since there were old men in the county in my own childhood who had actually seen it), stole an entire steamboat and had it dragged intact eleven miles overland to convert into a palace proper to aggrandise his state; the same fat black rich plantation earth still synonymous of the proud fading white plantation names whether we—*I mean of course they*—ever actually owned a plantation or not . . . (emphasis added, 278)

When Chick gazes down at the county, he sees the "earth which had bred his bones and those of his fathers" (*ID* 398); when Stevens gazes down he sees not that land but its history, and he cannot help superimposing himself upon it, projecting himself backwardly into it. Even as dark falls, Stevens claims, "there still remains one faint diffusion since everywhere you look about the dark panorama you still see them, faint as whispers" (278). Darkness, in fact, helps Stevens to clearly imagine the players in the legends of his Southern legacy even as those legends prevent him from accurately perceiving and effectively acting in the present.

• CHAPTER SIX •

"Forming Her Mind": Stevens and Linda Snopes Kohl

> I don't think that logic and intellect are the same thing. If I understand what logic means, it's to take a series of thoughts or ideas that continue to a logical conclusion. Or to a conclusion that is inevitable, assuming that one has stuck to the premise. Intellect is the business of taking that premise and following or fitting the next idea that fits it, the next idea that fits it, the next idea that fits it. There could be an error somewhere in that but the process of the intellect goes on.
>
> —William Faulkner (*LG* 109)

The Mansion continues Gavin Stevens's interest in Eula Varner Snopes's daughter, Linda Snopes Kohl. Stevens, hardly alone in his fascination, recognizes in Linda the difference that uniquely positions her among Faulkner's women as his most modern and controversial female character. Keith Louise Fulton defines Linda as Faulkner's "radical woman" (425) and Hee Kang sees in her a "new configuration of Faulkner's feminine" (21). Most relevant to my purposes, Diane Roberts describes Linda as an "anti-Belle" (140), a point Faulkner humorously makes when, in *The Mansion*, Linda forgets to allow Charles Mallison (apparently he has abandoned his childhood nickname of "Chick" by this time) to escort her to the door:

> Charles would have to get out fast . . . to get around the car in time. Though no matter how fast that was, she [Linda] would be already out, already turning up the walk toward the portico: who perhaps had left the South too young too long ago to have formed the Southern female habit-rite of a cavalier's unflagging constancy, or maybe the simple rivetting of ships had cured the old muscles of the old expectation. Whichever it was, Charles would have to overtake, in effect outrun her already halfway to the house; whereupon she would check, almost pause in fact, to glance back at him, startled—not alarmed: just startled; merely what Hollywood called a double-take, still not so far dis-severed from her Southern heritage but to recall that he, Charles, dared not risk some casual passerby reporting to his uncle that his nephew permitted the female he was seeing home to walk at least forty feet unaccompanied to her front door. (651-52)

Before her mother's death, Linda seems a fairly normal Yoknapatawphan teenager, well-schooled in and respectful of such cultural mores, but Eula's suicide understandably sets into motion many changes. After Eula dies, Linda leaves not for one of the northern colleges Gavin Stevens spends much of *The Town* lobbying for, but for Greenwich Village. Stevens tells Ratliff of the change in plans: "Too much has happened to her since. Too much, too fast, too quick. She outgrew colleges in about twenty-four hours two weeks ago. She'll have to grow back down to them again." Stevens adds, "Greenwich Village is the place for her" now because it is "a place with a few unimportant boundaries but no limitations where young people of any age go to seek dreams" (*T* 307). But Linda never "grows back down" to college. Although she is only nineteen, she leaves for New York at Stevens's urging, later meets and marries the communist Jewish sculptor, Barton Kohl, and the couple goes to Spain to fight with the Loyalists during the Spanish Civil War. Barton dies when his plane is shot down, and Linda, deafened by a shell that exploded near the ambulance she was driving, returns to Jefferson some ten years later (*M* 492).

Back in Mississippi, Linda continues to direct her revolutionary energies toward social and political causes. She begins "meddling with the Negroes" (*M* 531), working in the black schools and churches to improve education, and her efforts meet opposition from both the white and black communities of Yoknapatawpha; the principal of the local black school says to Stevens of Linda's ideas, "you are not ready for it yet and neither are we" (532). Ultimately, vandals targeting Flem's house move from merely chalking racial slurs on the sidewalk to setting afire "a crude cross soaked in gasoline" that "blazed suddenly on the lawn in front of the mansion" (535). Nevertheless, Linda continues with her efforts, "doing her Negro Sunday school classes" but "after a fashion condoned now, perhaps by familiarity and also that no one had discovered yet any way to stop her."[1] During "the rest of that spring and summer and fall of 1940 she was getting more and more restless," in part because of the escalating war in Europe. When she decides to take "a job, in a factory in California where they make aircraft to be sent to England and Russia," Stevens instead suggests that she work in the shipyard on the Mississippi Gulf Coast "*where they are building ships to carry airplanes guns tanks to help Russia*" (551, 552). Linda goes to Pascagoula and becomes "a riveter, where the deafness would be an actual advantage" (553).

When she again returns to Jefferson after the war, Charles thinks, "there was nothing for Linda to tilt against now in Jefferson. Come to think of it, there was nothing for her to tilt against anywhere now, since the Russians had fixed the Germans and even they didn't need her anymore" (*M* 645). Ratliff means much the same thing: "She has done run out of injustice. . . . So she will have to think of something, even if she has to invent it" (654). They indicate how clearly the people of Jefferson can see Linda's need to seek out and to participate in a crusade. This, of course, begs one overriding question: against what or whom does she really want, and perhaps even need, to wage war? Given the cause that she subsequently takes up, securing a pardon for Mink and the resulting murder of her *"so-called father"* (711), it would seem that she wants revenge against Flem. Ratliff implies as much when he wonders why Linda did not simply wait "two more years" until Mink finished serving his sentence and "God His-self couldn't a kept Mink in Parchman without He killed him" (717):

> Only she didn't [wait]. And so you wonder why. If maybe if there wasn't no folks in heaven it wouldn't be heaven, and if you couldn't recognise them as folks you knowed, wouldn't nobody want to go there. And that some day her maw would be saying to her, "Why didn't you revenge me and my love that I finally found it, instead of jest standing back and blind hoping for happen-so? Didn't you never have no love of your own to learn you what it is?" (717)

Ratliff's conjecture, though, fails to explain why Linda holds Flem responsible for her mother's death. Perhaps she just needs someone to blame and finds an easy target in Flem. Perhaps she remembers something from her childhood that motivates her response; after all, she surprises Stevens when she reveals her knowledge of her mother's affair shortly after Eula's suicide, remarking, "Oh yes, I knew about Manfred" (*T* 304). Or perhaps she hears some bit of gossip that makes her suspicious; Ratliff himself speculates that Eula "had her hair waved and her fingernails shined and went back home and presumably et supper or anyhow was present at it since it wasn't until about eleven oclock that *she seemed to taken up the pistol* and throwed the safety off" (emphasis added, *Mansion* 462). Ratliff's peculiar phrasing seems to question not that she "seemed to taken up" the pistol around eleven o'clock, but that she seemed to take it up, period, casting a hint of doubt on the circumstances of her death. At the very least, Ratliff believes that Flem thinks Linda has heard something that causes her to blame him, Flem, for her mother's death:

> Because naturally Flem cant walk right up to her and write on that tablet The minute you let that durn little water moccasin [Mink] out he's going to come straight back here and pay you up to date for your maw's grave and all the rest of it that these Jefferson meddlers has probably already persuaded you I was to blame for.... (665)

No one can know with certainty whether Linda hears this or any other gossip, but given that Eula's suicide would have provided much grist for the Yoknapatawphan rumor mill, it seems more likely than not that Linda would have been exposed to such talk, at least inadvertently.[2]

Whatever her reasons for targeting Flem, Linda surely learns much from watching him in action and from falling victim to his machinations herself. However, I would like to suggest that she learns just as much, if not more, from Stevens about the workings of the sort of "intellect" that Faulkner defines in this chapter's epigraph, and that Stevens, equally the target of her plan, equally deserves her rage.³ Linda doesn't "run out of injustice," as Ratliff thinks; she finally recognizes the irreparable damage that Stevens's meddling caused in her mother's life and her own.

When Stevens first begins spending time with Linda, "forming her mind," as he did with Melisandre Backus years before, Chick overhears his parents pondering Stevens's motives. His mother says "It's all right. . . . It's the same thing again: dont you remember? He never was really interested in Melisandre. I mean . . . . you know: really interested." She goes on to insist upon the innocence of Stevens's gifts, flowers and time spent reading poetry to Melisandre: "He was just forming her mind: that's all he wanted. And Melisandre was only five years younger, where with this one [Linda] he is twice her age, practically her grandfather. Of course that's all it is." Chick's father, however, will have none of it. Apparently in one of his less caustic moods, Charley only jokes, "Heh heh heh. Form is right, only it's on Gavin's mind, not hers. It would be on mine too if I wasn't already married and scared to look" (*T* 158). Many critics share Charley's belief; as Fulton puts it, Stevens's attention "fools only Linda" (428). I would add that he likely fools himself as well and probably does not fool Linda for long.

Stevens undoubtedly holds powerful sway over Linda in her youth and he does, in some sense, form her mind even as he surreptitiously minds her form, as Charley suggests. Eula even hints that Stevens's influence over Linda could potentially match Flem's in that the initial conflict between them erupted over the "school business":

> When you [Stevens] told her she wanted to go, get away from here; all the different schools to choose among that she hadn't even known about before, that it was perfectly natural for a young girl—young people to want to go to them and to go to one of them, that until then she hadn't even thought about, let alone known that she wanted to go to one of them. (*T* 282)

Eula, an undeniably shrewd judge of others by the time of *The Town*,⁴ makes it sound as if Stevens not only told Linda about these schools but also convinced her that she wanted to go because the desire to escape "was perfectly natural." Fulton describes Stevens's influence over Linda in light of his involuntary role as "Flem's model, teacher, and accomplice":

> He [Stevens] will teach Linda to value love whether it exists or not and Flem will trade on that "love" to obtain her inheritance. Gavin will see to it that the suicide Eula is

buried respectably, covering in her death the cause of it. When he commissions a marble medallion from Italy to mark Eula's grave, he blocks in marble the woman Flem has bought and cashed in (although he does so in part because that is the price to be paid for Linda's freedom). (430)[5]

In *The Mansion*, the mature Charles similarly alludes to the danger of following Stevens blindly, a lesson he has likely learned from personal experience, when he says of his uncle, "he is a good man. Maybe I was wrong sometimes to trust and follow him but I was never wrong to love him" (538).

Although well-intentioned, Stevens's actions in the days following Eula's death teach Linda devastating lessons. Most obviously she learns, from Stevens's example, of the damage that even a well-meaning lie can cause. Chapter twenty-two of *The Town* consists solely of Stevens and Linda's conversation about her parentage; therein, she never asks Stevens if Flem is her father, but simply states, "He's not my father." Stevens responds, "Certainly he is. What in the world are you talking about? . . . Do you want me to swear? All right. I swear he's your father" (304). But Stevens swears to the wrong thing at the wrong time; readers who remember his swearing to Eula that he will marry Linda if "nothing else but marrying me can help her" (292) realize that Stevens's promises hold little value. Linda allows herself to believe Stevens by rationalizing that he is "the one person in the world I know will never lie to me" (304) and Stevens remains, as Fulton notes, "Gallantly consistent" when he "insists to Linda from the beginning that Flem is her father." Linda realizes that Stevens lies to protect her only "after she has been victimized—in part because he [Stevens] has lied to her. Child that she was, she put real feeling into a false story of kinship and love" (430). Fulton's use of the term "victimized," of course, refers to Flem's manipulation of Linda's filial affection to gain leverage over Eula. However, Linda equally falls victim to Stevens's good intentions, specifically those motivating his lie about her parentage, that make her even more vulnerable to Flem's power.

Stevens, perhaps again with the best of intentions, also models the use of courtesy as a weapon. Faulkner demonstrates on several occasions that Stevens can adroitly manipulate others with the cudgel of courtesy by using refined manners to get what he wants. In one instance, he acts in such fashion to convince his sister to secure an invitation for the Snopeses to the Cotillion Club's Christmas ball; as Chick observes, Stevens never missed "a chance to do things for Mother, he even invented little things to do for her, so that even when he would talk a little, it was like he was killing two birds with the same stone" (*T* 45). He does not have difficulty securing Maggie's help; Chick notices that she will not let her twin brother suffer when "she could help and fend him" (*T* 268). He manipulates Linda's affections just as easily, most notably when they talk about her plans for college just before Stevens meets again with Eula: "Of course I dont really need to ask you this, but maybe we'd better just for the record. You dont really want to stay in Jefferson, do you? You really do want to go up East to school?" Stevens then almost immediately continues, "All right, I take that back. I cant ask you that; I cant ask you to say outright you want to go against your mother" (191). Although Stevens ostensibly utters this speech because Linda's hat, as he reflects, "reminded me of that only other time I ever saw her in a hat which was that fiasco of a Sunday dinner at home two years ago which was the first time I compelled, forced her to do something because she didn't know how to refuse" (191). He essentially repeats that offense by refusing to allow her to speak, either against or in support of her mother. Stevens simply decides that Linda does not "want to be there" when he talks to Eula, and begins to plan accordingly when she utters an ambiguous "No. No" (191-92). In fact, Stevens can even discard his polite ways if necessary, as he does when trying to convince Eula to allow Linda to "go away from Jefferson to school." After Eula reveals Flem's objections, Stevens asks, "But why? . . . Why? When she's not even his [Flem's]—he's not even her—I'm sorry. But you can see how urgent, how we dont even have time for . . . . ." Eula finishes his comment by saying, "Politeness?" (196).

While it seems that Stevens knows little about what Linda wants or needs, even as a teenager, Faulkner makes clear that the adult Linda understands Stevens as fully as her mother did before her.[6] As a child, Linda thought of Stevens as "the one person in the world I know will never lie to me" (*T* 304); she has matured enough by the time of *The Mansion* to more accurately "love" Stevens because "every time you [Stevens] lie to me I can always know you will stick to it" (489). In *The Town* Ratliff indicates that Stevens "never understood her [Eula] and never would," and then adds:

> And he never did realise that she [Eula] understood him because she never had no way of telling him because she didn't know herself how she done it. Since women learn at about two or three years old and then forget it, the knowledge about theirselves that a man stumbles on by accident forty-odd years later with the same kind of startled amazement of finding a twenty-five cent piece in a old pair of britches you had started to throw away. (88)

Most obviously, Linda recognizes Stevens's romantic bent, just as her mother discerned his need for "the poet's romantic dream" of ideal love (199). For example, when Stevens awaits Eula's first visit he thinks:

> I was simply waiting for those two hundred nights [that he spent longing for Eula] to culminate as I had spent at least some of them or some small part of them expecting when this moment came, if it did, would, was fated: I to be swept up as into storm or hurricane or tornado itself and tossed wrung and wrenched and consumed, the light

last final spent insentient husk to float slowing and weightless, for a moment longer during the long vacant rest of life, and then no more. (80-81)

Stevens longs to "be swept up" and consumed by a grand passion, but "it didn't happen" (T 81). Or, rather, it did not happen with the ever-practical Eula because her forthrightness precluded such nonsense. Linda, though, "has the complexity of mythological thought yet represents a twist to our comprehension of mythology" (Fulton 432):

> Although he [Faulkner] gives the last words to a description of Mink and his dying into the earth, in Linda he realizes the power with which she derives out of the story into life. In the tradition of male writers investing female characters with qualities precluded by their ideas of masculinity, Faulkner creates a female survivor, an Athena, whose quacking voice offers no rhetorical justification of the law and whose actions name the mother. Linda is not born solely from the head of her creator but, like the warrior Athena, transformed from earlier figures; women fighting for freedom and equality are perhaps Faulkner's hope and our own. In Linda, his fictional vessel of life, Faulkner sends his radical vision out of the story and into the future. (435-36)

Roberts quite rightly points out that "the operative myth for Gavin" in his relationship with Linda "must be Pygmalion and Galatea. Gavin thinks he is 'making' the perfect woman; yet when she comes to life and comes of age, she has a mind and a will of her own" (142). Linda not only "has a mind and a will of her own" but also relies on the traditional myths Stevens has taught her and uses this knowledge, along with all she has learned about him, to co-opt the role of Pygmalion. Linda proves herself Stevens's most adept protégé as she exploits his romantic bent and even turns him into an accomplice to murder. Before she leaves for Pascagoula, she offers herself to Stevens even more boldly than her mother did. Stevens ostensibly recalls her proposal as a direct quotation, but he cannot bring himself to record, even as a euphemism or with a blank space, the four-letter word Linda uses to refer to intercourse that shocks him so: "'But you can me,' she said. That's right. She used the explicit word, speaking the hard brutal guttural."[7] The horrified Stevens actually blushes at Linda's frank language and when she asks him to tell her what other word he prefers he writes on her tablet:

> There is no other thats the right one only one I am old fashioned it still shocks me a little No what shocks is when a woman uses it & is not shocked at all until she realises I am Then I wrote: thats wrong too what shocks is that all that magic passion excitement be summed up & dismissed in that one bald unlovely sound. . . . (M 546)

After shocking Stevens far more than her mother did, Linda agrees to share his vision of chivalric love; she agrees that they can continue to exist as "the only two people in the world that love each other and dont have to" (548). Most scholars presume that some physical expression of love constitutes the logical completion of this line. Nancy Norris, for example, speculates, "Surely the end of her infinitive was 'make love'" (230).[8] A scant ten pages later, Linda even plays the role that Eula never would when she joins Stevens in his mythmaking during his visit to Pascagoula. When he arrives, Linda sets the stage, beginning with a sunset stroll on the beach. As they face "the moment's pause before the final plunge of the sun," Linda connects the past to the present in a speech that Stevens could easily have uttered:

> It's all right now. We were here. We saved it. Used it. I mean, for the earth to have come all this long way from the beginning of the earth, and the sun to have come all this way from beginning of time, for this one day and minute and second out of all the days and minutes and seconds, and nobody to use it, no two people who are finally together at last after all the difficulties and waiting, and now they are together at last and are desperate because of all the long waiting, they are even running along the beach toward where the place is, not far now, where they will finally be alone together at last and nobody in the world to know or care or interfere so that it's like the world itself wasn't except you so now the world that wasn't even invented yet can begin. (M 554-55)

After creating this vision of herself and Stevens as Eve and Adam-like figures transcending all time, Linda invokes yet another myth when she secures two adjoining hotel rooms so that she and Stevens can act out their own version of the story of Pyramus and Thisbe. She tells Stevens that she wants him to marry another because "then it will be all right. We can always be together no matter how far apart either one of us happens to be or has to be" (558).[9] She then kisses him and tells him to "go back home" tomorrow morning. Stevens protests that he "*was going to Stay all day*" and Linda replies:

> No. Tomorrow. Early. I'll put my hand on the wall and when you're in bed knock on it and if I wake up in the night I can knock and if you're awake or still there you can knock back and if I dont feel you knock you can write me from Jefferson tomorrow or the next day. Because I'm all right now. Good night, Gavin. (559)

In Ovid's tale, from which Shakespeare draws in *Romeo and Juliet* and stages as a play within a play in *A Midsummer Night's Dream*, Thisbe and Pyramus, the children of two warring houses, similarly communicate via a crack in the wall that separates their two residences. One night, the two agree to meet outside the city at the Tomb of Ninus, but a lion frightens Thisbe away. She drops her veil, the lion tears it and smears blood from a fresh kill on it, and Pyramus arrives and draws the logical conclusion. He kills himself, and she returns to find his body. In consequence, she kills herself. Faulkner's use of this story seems particularly apropos because it takes place during the rule of Semiramis, whom Faulkner often identifies with Eula.[10]

Whether or not Linda has already thought of murdering Flem at this point, she ensures Stevens's complicity in her plan by catering to his fantasies;

in doing so, she reveals the destruction of those fantasies that enable Stevens's willful innocence as her ultimate goal, a goal to which Flem is perhaps even incidental. As Ratliff repeatedly points out, sooner or later Flem will die by Mink's hand, and Mink himself thinks of his mission: "*If a feller jest wants to do something, he might make it and he might not. But if he's GOT to do something, cant nothing stop him*" (M 375). Linda simply arranges to have that something happen sooner by orchestrating Mink's release. More importantly, by allowing Stevens to discover that she acted with forethought, she forces him to acknowledge her participation in Flem's death. In doing so, she attempts to make him realize his own role as well and admit the danger and idiocy of his refusal to face the reality of a world in which he continues to take actions that have devastating consequences. Sometime between leaving for New York at Stevens's urging, marrying a man perhaps even more idealistic than Stevens, and returning to Jefferson after the second World War, Linda finally recognizes the very real danger posed by Stevens's romantic illusions.[11] She at last learns the message that Charles tried to pass on to her through Stevens, one that Faulkner seems to have learned from experiences connected to his own public stances on political and racial issues in the 1950s:

> when I got home that Christmas I said to Gavin: "Tell her to tear up that goddamn [communist] party card, if she's got one. Go on. Tell her. She cant help people. They are not worth it. They dont want to be helped any more than they want advice or work. They want cake and excitement, both free. Man stinks. How the hell can she have spent a year in a war that not only killed her husband and blew the bejesus out of the inside of her skull, but even at that price the side she was fighting for still lost, without finding that out? Oh sure, I know, I know, you and Ratliff both have told me often enough; if I've heard Ratliff one time I've heard him a hundred: 'Man ain't really evil, he jest aint got any sense.' But so much the more reason, because that leaves him completely hopeless, completely worthless of anybody's anguish and effort and trouble." (537-38)

Charles stops speaking when Stevens, falling into an old pattern of behavior, "put his hand on my head. He had to reach up to do it now, but he did it exactly as he used to when I was half as tall and only a third as old" and says, "Why dont you tell her?" (538). Charles apologizes for his outburst, but only after thinking of Stevens:

> he is a good man, wise too except for the occasions when he would aberrate, go momentarily haywire and take a wrong turn that even I could see was wrong, and then go hell-for-leather, with absolutely no deviation from logic and rationality from there on, until he wound us up in a mess or trouble or embarrassment that even I would have had sense enough to dodge. (538)

Given his description of Stevens's wrong-headed, undeviating pursuits quite similar to the progression Faulkner defines in this chapter's epigraph, it would seem that Charles apologizes not for his words, but for offending Stevens's sensibilities.[12]

Linda, now far past such concerns, may very well blame Flem for manipulating her own life and ending her mother's, but she quite rightly blames Stevens as well and orchestrates Mink's release in hopes of forcing Stevens to accept responsibility for his destructive, meddling ways. Stevens, though, clings tenaciously to his illusions; indeed, he ludicrously thinks of writing to Linda near the end of *The Mansion*, "*I have everything. You trusted me. You chose to let me find you murdered your so-called father rather than tell me a lie.*" He thinks that he "could" and "perhaps should" write, "*I have everything. Haven't I just finished being accessory before a murder.*" Instead, he chooses the romantic middle ground and simply writes, "*We have had everything*" (M 711), when, actually, he has nothing save his impossible dreams and a handkerchief stained with the lipstick of Linda's last kiss locked in a drawer in his office (713).

Stevens may finally begin to enter into a more complex state of moral awareness in *The Mansion* as Joseph R. Urgo suggests (*Apocrypha* 200). If so, Linda forces such realization, and his actions belie his words to show that he hardly attains any measurable level of self-actualization before novel's end. For example, about two-thirds of the way through *The Mansion*, Charles reveals how little his uncle's attitudes about truth and justice have evolved:

> Uncle Gavin always said he was not really interested in truth nor even in justice: that all he wanted was just to know, to find out, whether the answer was any of his business or not; and that all means to that end were valid, provided he left neither hostile witnesses nor incriminating evidence. Charles didn't believe him; some of his methods were not only too hard, they took too long; and there are some things you simply do not do even to find out. But his uncle said that he, Charles, was wrong: that curiosity is another of the mistresses whose slaves decline no sacrifice. (638)

Stevens connects that curiosity to his profession more concretely when he tells Linda that he was "*happy*" to have been "*given the privilege of meddling with impunity in other peoples affairs without really doing any harm by belonging to that avocation whose acolytes have been absolved in advance for holding justice above truth*" (656). Stevens, though, foolishly continues to hold curiosity above all else, regardless of whether he does harm or not; when Mink leaves Parchman without the money that requires him to stay away from Jefferson, Stevens anxiously waits for Ratliff to return from the penitentiary because "what he really wanted with Ratliff was to find out how Mink had . . . got past the Parchman gate without that absolutely contingent money." Moreover, Stevens wants to know how Mink "managed it in such a way that apparently only the absolutely unpredicted and unwarranted presence of Ratliff at a place and time that he had no business whatever being, revealed the fact that he hadn't taken it" (672-73).

Stevens may say, "There aren't any morals," and "People just do the best they can" (M 715), but he nevertheless refuses to abandon his willful ignorance as it concerns Linda and allow that she, too, simply acts as best she can given the circumstances. Instead, Stevens focuses on his role in the events. When he kisses Linda for the last time, he thinks that he would normally touch her, "learning and knowing not with despair or grief but just sorrow a little, simply supporting her buttocks as you cup the innocent hipless bottom of a child. But not now, not this time. It was terror now" (710). Rather than acknowledging that terror and its source, he goes on to cast himself "with terror" in the role of a doomed hero in some unspecific myth that resembles the tale of Gawain's marriage to Dame Ragnelle:

> How did it go? the man 'whose irresistible attraction to women was that simply by being in their presence he gave them to convince themselves that he was capable of any sacrifice for them.' Which is backward, completely backward; the poor dope not only didn't know where first base was, he didn't know he was playing baseball. You dont need to tempt them because they have long since already selected you by that time, choosing you simply because they believe that in the simple act of being selected you have at once become not merely willing and ready but passionately desirous of making a sacrifice for them just as soon as the two of you can think of one good enough, worthy. (710)[13]

Stevens also tells Ratliff as they prepare to deliver Linda's cash to Mink, "I'm not safe." Ratliff, thinking Stevens means that he, Stevens, is not safe, replies, "It's all over now, soon that is as we get used to it." Stevens, inflating his own importance (and thus deflecting blame from Linda, at least in his own mind), clarifies, "I mean, you're not safe. Nobody is, around me. I'm dangerous. Cant you understand I've just committed murder?" Ratliff replies with typical aplomb, "Oh, that" (713), and goes on to liken Linda's plan to kill Flem to a game, one quite similar to the exchange that the Green Knight proposes to Arthur's court. Ratliff realizes that as a "town-raised" boy, Stevens probably never played this game, "Give-me-lief," so Ratliff describes it for him:

> You would pick out another boy about your own size and you would walk up to him with a switch or maybe a light stick or a hard green apple or maybe even a rock, depending on how hard a risk you wanted to take, and say to him, 'Gimme lief,' and if he agreed, he would stand still and you would take one cut or one lick at him with the switch or stick, as hard as you picked out, or back off and throw at him once with the green apple or the rock. Then you would stand still and he would take the same switch or stick or apple or rock or anyways another one jest like it, and take one cut or throw at you. That was the rule. (716)

Ratliff then constructs the analogy between this child's game and the conflict between Linda and Flem:

"So jest suppose—"
"Drive on!" Stevens said.

> "—Flem had had his lief fair and square like the rule said, so there wasn't nothing for him to do but jest set there, since he had likely found out years back when she finally turned up here again even outen a communist war, that he had already lost—"
> "Stop it!" Stevens said. "Dont say it!"
> "—and now it was her lief and so suppose—"
> "No!" Stevens said. "No!" But Ratliff was not only nearer the switch, his hand was already on it, covering it.
> "—she knowed all the time what was going to happen when he [Mink] got out, that not only she knowed but Flem did too—"
> "I wont believe it!" Stevens said. "I wont! I cant believe it," he said. "Dont you see I cannot?" (716)

Ratliff, like Linda, refuses to "give" Stevens "lief." He points out that Linda acted deliberately to avenge her mother's death and took an active role in Flem's murder by securing Mink's pardon, even though the situation would have almost certainly played out in much the same fashion when Mink finished serving his sentence in another two years. Ratliff's observation presumably reduces Stevens to tears because Ratliff "took out the immaculately clean, impeccably laundered and ironed handkerchief which the town said he not only laundered himself but hemstitched himself too, and put it into Stevens' blind hand and turned the switch and flicked on the headlights" (717). Stevens refuses to see the metaphorical light that Ratliff tries to bring to the situation and continues to do Linda's bidding by delivering the cash to Mink along with the promise that more will follow (718).

In *The Mansion*, we see Linda a final time as she cuts the last of her ties to Jefferson; she gives Stevens the cash for Mink and the deed to the de Spain house, "turned and went to the door and stopped and half-turned and only then looked at him: no faint smile, no nothing: just the eyes which even at this distance were not quite black. Then she was gone" (712). Linda charges Stevens with two legal tasks, neither of which bears completion—transferring the cash to Mink and giving Flem's mansion back to the de Spain family. The first makes Stevens an accessory before and after the fact of Flem's murder, the second only complicates matters for de Spain's relatives. As Ratliff elaborates:

> And now all that's left of it is for a bed-rode old lady and her retired old maid schoolteacher daughter that would a lived happily ever after in sunny golden California. But now they got to come all the way back to Mississippi and live in that-ere big white elephant of a house where likely Miss Allison will have to go back to work again, maybe even have to hump and hustle some to keep it up since how can they have mere friends and acquaintances, let alone strangers, saying how a Mississippi-born and-bred lady refused to accept a whole house not only gift-free-for-nothing but that was actively theirn anyhow to begin with, without owing even much obliged to nobody for getting it back. (714-15)

Ratliff surmises, "Maybe there's even a moral in it somewhere, if you jest knowed where to look" (715). The moral that even Ratliff misses (or perhaps just refuses to articulate) involves Stevens's utter failure of Linda's final test. She gives him one last chance to do the right thing rather than the romantic one, and he fulfills her parting wishes against surely even his better judgment.

We last see Stevens as he and Ratliff leave Mink. In this scene the narrator suggests a similarity between the three men, describing Ratliff and Stevens as "two old men themselves, approaching their sixties" (M 719). Faulkner links them to Mink again in the glorious language of the novel's conclusion. As Mink presumably prepares to die and imagines his life seeping "down and down into the ground already full of the folks that had the trouble but were free now" (720), Faulkner writes:

> it was just the ground and the dirt that had to bother and worry and anguish with the passions and hopes and skeers, the justice and the injustice and the griefs, leaving the folks themselves easy now, all mixed and jumbled up comfortable and easy so wouldn't nobody even know or even care who was which anymore, himself among them, equal to any, good as any, brave as any, being inextricable from, anonymous with all of them: the beautiful, the splendid, the proud and the brave, right on up to the very top itself among the shining phantoms and dreams which are the milestones of the long human recording—Helen and the bishops, the kings and the unhomed angels, the scornful and graceless seraphim. (720-21)

Many scholars, such as George Garrett, read this excerpt as Mink's "final and authentic vision of himself among the dead" (xii), but it also functions as a passage of free indirect discourse shared between Mink and some unnamed narrative voice, perhaps even Faulkner's, and while Mink may very well share the sentiment of the conclusion, it seems virtually impossible that he would articulate it in such eloquent fashion given what Faulkner reveals of his speech and thought processes. Woodrow Stroble notes that these final lines make "Mink—*and Flem*—equal with everyone at the end of the trilogy" and recognizes that "an ethical evaluation is constantly evoked by the internal narrators, but that it is Faulkner's evaluation cannot be claimed" (210). I would add that the conclusion also implicitly equates Stevens, and, more importantly, the very stuff of his dreams with the murderous Mink, a circumstance that perhaps comes as close to any sort of ethical evaluation as Faulkner found himself willing to venture.

While at the University of Virginia, Faulkner described Stevens as a "knight that goes out to defend somebody who don't want to be defended and don't need it" (*FU* 141), such as when he tragicomically tries to "protect" Linda from the knowledge of Mink's botched release when she has already helped Mink escape after he shot Flem (M 684). Stevens even later thinks of Linda, "*Why should she waste her time trusting me when she has known all her life that all she has to do is just depend on me*" (710). Linda does not have to depend on Stevens in such fashion, and she certainly does not need his dubious protection. Of course, Faulkner's assessment also means that Stevens neglects those who most need defending, as when he stands up for Eula at the Christmas ball in *The Town* yet fails to act later when she so desperately needs rescuing. Faulkner suggests that Stevens reacts as he does because he "had got out of his depth" in *The Town*:

> He got into a real world in which people anguished and suffered, not simply did things which they shouldn't do. And he wasn't as prepared to cope with people who were following their own bent, not for a profit but simply because they had to. That is, he knew a good deal less about people than he knew about the law and about ways of evidence and drawing the right conclusions from what he saw with his legal mind. When he had to deal with people, he was an amateur. (*FU* 140)

Stevens certainly gets out of his depth in his last meeting with Linda: "She just stood holding him and kissing him until he himself moved first to be free. Then she released him and stood looking at his face out of the dark blue eyes not secret, not tender, perhaps not even gentle" (*M* 710). The narrator speculates shortly thereafter, "someday perhaps he [Stevens] would remember that they had never been really tender even" (711), but such a realization seems unlikely. Ratliff, ever the astute judge of Stevens, observes, "It wasn't that he was born too soon or too late or even in the wrong place. He was born at exactly the right time, only in the wrong envelope" (*M* 446). Indeed an amateur until the very end, Stevens remains perhaps Faulkner's most errant knight and certainly his most deluded. Firmly encased in "that fragile and . . . gossamer-sinewed envelope of boundless and hopeless aspiration Old Moster give him" (446), Stevens will forever quest after a dream that he dooms in the dreaming of it.

• CHAPTER SEVEN •

Conclusion: "A Gentleman Can Live Through Anything"

> I would say if there is one truth of the human heart, it would be to believe in itself, believe in its capacity to aspire, to be better than it is, might be.
>
> —William Faulkner (*FU* 78)

In his last novel, *The Reivers*, Faulkner presents a final knight in training, a gentleman squire of sorts in the person of Lucius Priest.[1] Near the novel's conclusion, Lucius's grandfather tries to teach him what Gavin Stevens never learns: "A gentleman can live through anything. He faces anything. A gentleman accepts the responsibility of his actions and bears the burden of their consequences, even when he did not himself instigate them but only acquiesced to them, didn't say No though he knew he should" (969). Faulkner provides us with reason to believe that Lucius's courage, sensitivity, and innate moral sensibility allow him to learn such a lesson. When he first mentioned the idea for this novel to Robert K. Haas in a letter dated May 3, 1940, Faulkner described it as "a sort of Huck Finn" story about

> a normal boy of about twelve or thirteen, a big, warmhearted, courageous, honest, utterly unreliable white man with the mentality of a child, an old negro family servant, opinionated, querulous, selfish, fairly unscrupulous, and in his second childhood, and a prostitute not very young anymore and with a great deal of character and generosity and common sense, and a stolen race horse which none of them actually intended to steal. (*SL* 123)

Faulkner added, "The story lasts a matter of weeks. During that time the boy grows up, becomes a man, and a good man, mostly because of the influence of the whore." Lucius "goes through in miniature all the experiences of youth which mold the man's character." Even though these experiences "stand for debauchery and degeneracy and actual criminality" in "his middle class parents' eyes," through "them he learned courage and honor and generosity and pride and pity" (123-24).

Of course, Faulkner changed some of the details before he wrote to Albert Erskine in October of 1961 that he had finished the manuscript of *The Reivers* (*SL* 456); for example, the story lasts a matter of days rather than weeks and Lucius is eleven rather than thirteen when it takes place. However, what Lucius learns from the experience and from his grandfather remains the same, and only the time that Faulkner did not have would have told whether or not Lucius continued to heed his grandfather's words as he matured. Random House published *The Reivers* in June of 1962, and Faulkner died a mere month later, leaving behind no plan for another novel. Joseph R. Urgo writes that, as the title indicates, the "book is about stealing: stealing guns, stealing cars, stealing horses, and most significantly, stealing experience and meaning from those in control of such phenomena" ("*Reivers*" 317).[2] Urgo adds that the idea of this "experiential reiving is masked in the novel beneath a narrative that verges on the trivial and harmless" (318). Lucius tells the deceptively simple tale to his own grandson almost sixty years after the events occurred, and Grandfather / Lucius, as Urgo points out, warns against "making him [Grandfather / Lucius] into the kind of icon that prohibits, or even inhibits, future creation" (317).

The final lines of *The Reivers* also suggest that in Lucius, Faulkner created a different sort of gentleman, one molded both by personal instinct and by his grandfather's influence. As the novel ends, we learn that Boon and Corrie (or Everbe Corinthia) name their son "Lucius Priest Hoggenbeck." This child that Lucius describes as "just another baby, already as ugly as Boon even if it would have to wait twenty years to be as big" (971), testifies to the debt the couple feels they owe Lucius, a repayment for his role in helping to cement their relationship. Lucius first becomes involved when Corrie vows to quit working as a prostitute after he gallantly fights her fifteen-year-old nephew, Otis, to defend her honor; she tells Lucius, "You fought because of me. I've had people—drunks—fighting over me, but you're the first one ever fought for me." After the fight, Boon marvels that he is only eleven years old and "already knife-cut in a whore house brawl." He then says, "I wish I had knowed you thirty years ago. With you to learn me when I was eleven years old, maybe by this time I'd a had some sense too" (854). Boon's ironic comment, though, also looks ahead to what he learns from Lucius about the possibility for a future with Corrie, regardless of her past, because of her basic goodness and inherent worth. Michael Millgate identified Lucius as "the instrument of her [Corrie's] reformation" early on (*Achievement* 254), and Urgo adds that Boon too "is transformed by the realization of his capacity to refuse" to accept his life as it is ("*Reivers*" 318). Boon seems to credit Lucius with that realization when he tells Boss and Lucius that he does indeed plan to marry Corrie: "God damn it, . . . if you [Lucius] can go bare-handed against a knife defending her, why the hell cant I marry her? Aint I as good as you are, even if I aint eleven years old?" (966). As Olga W. Vickery puts it in her reading that describes the world of *The Reivers* as an "enchanted land" in which "the knight must win his lady not by offering money but by overcoming all obstacles and defeating all challengers" (228, 234):

> Through love . . . Boon is changed from an unrestrained, lustful male to a knight in shining armor. He claims Everbe Corinthia not because of his conquest of others but because he has conquered himself. He is willing to devote whatever he is or has become to her love and service. In so doing he gains certain magical powers; for if Lucius could make Everbe a virtuous woman, Boon can transform her into a wife, and that transformation which signals the conventional happy ending is accepted not only by the "reivers" but by Jefferson as well. (235)[3]

The passage in which Uncle Parsham teaches Lucius to "drive a mule to a buggy" offers a useful gloss on Lucius's influence over Boon. Uncle Parsham says:

> A mule aint like a horse. When a horse gets a wrong notion in his head, all you got to do is swap him another one for it. Most anything will do—a whip or spur or just scare him by hollering at him. A mule is different. He can hold two notions at the same time and the way to change one of them is to act like you believe he thought of changing it first. He'll know different, because mules have got sense. But a mule is a gentleman too, and when you act courteous and respectful at him without trying to buy him or scare him, he'll act courteous and respectful back at you—as long as you dont overstep him. That's why you dont pet a mule like you do a horse: he knows you dont love him: you're just trying to fool him into doing something he already dont aim to do, and it insults him. Handle him like that. He knows the way home, and he will know it aint me holding the lines. So all you need to do is tell him with the lines that you know the way too but he lives here and you're just a boy so you want him to go in front. (923)[4]

Lucius soon "could feel what Uncle Parsham meant" and recalls, "there came back to me through the lines not just power, but intelligence, sagacity; not just the capacity but the willingness to choose when necessary between two alternatives and to make the right decision without hesitation" (923). Lucius's respect for Corrie, expressed by his defense of her, helps Boon to make a choice similar to the one Uncle Parsham forces upon the mule. Thus Lucius inadvertently teaches Boon another lesson he ostensibly learned from his grandfather, but one he must have already known on some level: "now I knew what Grandfather meant: that your outside is just what you live in, sleep in, and has little connection with who you are and even less with what you do" (R 970). Lucius is not concerned with trappings of grandeur or idealistic notions about the nature of humankind; he is concerned with doing the right thing, and he knows that the past four days have changed him:

if all that [the events of the past four days] had changed nothing, was the same as if it had never been—nothing smaller or larger or older or wiser or more pitying—then something had been wasted, thrown away, spent for nothing; either it was wrong or false to begin with and should never have existed, or I was wrong and false or weak or anyway not worthy of it. (967)

Faulkner often spoke in a similar fashion of a man's desire to "be better than he is afraid he might be" (*FU* 86) and Lucius represents the best of that human impulse. In the end, Faulkner's final gentleman possesses humility, stands capable of and desirous of learning, and knows, as Faulkner did, that the fiercest demons, the ones that require a knight's true courage, always reside within our own hearts and minds.

Notes

Chapter One

1. Many scholars have drawn such biographical comparisons, including Cleanth Brooks, Louis D. Rubin, Jr., Lewis P. Simpson, John T. Irwin, and Jeffrey J. Folks, just to name a few. See, for example, Lothar Hönnighausen's discussion of these figures as "cruel self-caricatures" in chapter four of *Faulkner: Masks and Metaphors* (112).
2. André Bleikasten adds, "No novelist has been more alert to the ambiguities and perils of idealism than Faulkner; no one has shown greater insight into its murky origins and motivations, its insidious destructiveness, its secret affinity with evil and death" (38).
3. Stevens appears in seven novels and short story collections and in various short stories, some of which Faulkner revised and incorporated into those novels and collections, and some which he did not. For an exhaustive list of these appearances, see Mary Montgomery Dunlap's appendix.
4. For instance, M.C. Flannery and John G. Cawelti identify Stevens as "Faulkner's Favorite" and determine that "he is certainly more a spokesman for Faulkner than any other character in the Yoknapatawpha saga" (22).
5. In *A Fable*, Faulkner rewrites the major narrative of modern western civilization, the crucifixion of Christ, thus continuing the modernist enterprise of rewriting old cultural myths to fit the twentieth century. As Joseph R. Urgo puts it, Faulkner "recreates the life of Christ in his own time" as he "claims in *A Fable* to witness and narrate a recasting of the challenge, passion, and condemnation of the Child of God" (*Apocrypha* 95). After working on the novel for over ten years, Faulkner published it in 1954; Polk points out that "Faulkner's continued work on *A Fable* forms a steady ground bass for all his other activities, public and private" throughout this period ("Polysyllabic" 318).
6. See Carl S. Singleton and Flannery and Cawelti.

Chapter Two

1. These are just a few such references. For others see *Faulkner in the University*, *Lion in the Garden*, and Faulkner's *Selected Letters*.
2. At least the Faulkners still owned their home at 917 Rugby Road in April 1962. Joseph Blotner reports that at that time, "The Faulkners were now staying with Jill and Paul [Summers]. They had placed their Rugby Road home on the market and were seeking a place in the country" (*SL* 460). Blotner describes that place, Red Acres, as "250 of the most beautiful acres in the Piedmont, not far from Farmington and the Blue Ridge" (*A Biography*

[1984] 701). The Faulkners presumably still owned the home on Rugby Road when Faulkner died; Blotner purchased the house from Mrs. Faulkner in 1965 and continued to work on Faulkner's biography while living there (Blotner, "Mr. Faulkner" 338).

3   Thadious M. Davis points out that Faulkner even interrogated whiteness in this context: "One measure of Faulkner's enormous literary achievement is his construction of race as central to his fiction, to his representation of characters, specifically his construction of white characters and whiteness, and to the metaphorical power of his language struggling with an interrogation of what it means to be white. That achievement is remarkable for its insistent race consciousness, for enabling discourses on race and racial transgressions and transactions not merely in the South but in the United States as a whole. This particular aspect of his achievement is not usually acknowledged primarily because most attention has been devoted to his construction of racial Others, the African Americans and to a lesser extent the Native Americans who populate his texts. This discourse is particularly salient, not merely because it disturbs the notion that race only applies to people of color in Faulkner's writing, but also because it constitutes one of the possibilities for fresh conversations about Faulkner's particular achievement and the potential for future Faulkner scholarship" (208).

4   Richard A. Milum carefully traces the roots and various manifestations of the figure in Faulkner's fiction. For excellent discussions of the influence of the romance genre on Southern literature see Ellen Weinauer's entry for "Romance Genre" in *The Companion to Southern Literature* and G.R. Thompson's essay, "Edgar Allan Poe and the Writers of the Old South."

5   See F. Garvin Davenport, Jr. for a more detailed description of typical Cavalier characteristics.

6   The narrator of *Flags in the Dust* reports that Montgomery Ward Snopes "departed with Horace to a position in the Y.M.C.A." (679). In *The Town*, Chick Mallison says that Montgomery Ward "came to Uncle Gavin, to go to France with Uncle Gavin in the Y.M.C.A." (92). See Irwin for a discussion of Horace Benbow "as a transitional figure between Quentin Compson and Gavin Stevens" ("Horace Benbow" 544).

7   I do not mean to imply, of course, that Hightower is not connected to Blount. Michael Millgate first suggested that in "Rose of Lebanon" Blount "directly prefigured" Hightower, as he certainly does (*Achievement* 130). The Memphis stories include "The Big Shot," revised as "Dull Tale," and "Rose of Lebanon," revised as "A Return." See Robert Woods Sayre for information about the composition and publication histories of these stories.

8   See chapter three for a discussion of Stevens's theories on race.

9   As Deiter Meindl points out, though, "Gavin is probably wide off the mark in explaining that she [Randolph] gave up the derringer because in having uttered an obscenity, 'she found she didn't deserve to be protected by a clean bullet'" (588).

10 Also in this instance Ratliff (rather than Stevens, as is usually the case) misreads the situation between Hawkshaw and Susan Reed. As Hans H. Skei points out, "The story about Hawkshaw and Susan Reed is the product of the narrator's rather limited total understanding, and yet there is more to it than this. The narrator reveals some of his prejudice, and the denouement shows that he has misinterpreted everything that he has watched and speculated on" (*Novelist* 176).

11 Stephen E. Meats adds that Faulkner's "hand-drawn map of Yoknapatawpha County which appears in *Absalom, Absalom!*" and "identifies Joanna Burden's house as the place 'where Christmas killed Miss Burden'" leaves "little ground for disputing" that Christmas killed her (277). Still, as Meats points out, "there is no positive evidence in the novel to indicate who actually commits the murder. We have only the fact of the murder itself" (271).

12 The most obvious such passages include Ratliff's refrain concerning Stevens's incomprehension of Flem Snopes in *The Town*: he "missed it" (135, 226). Other examples include Ratliff's belief that "Lawyer Stevens never understood her [Eula] and never would" (88) and his prediction in *The Mansion* that Linda "aint going to marry him [Stevens]. It's going to be worse than that" (562).
13 For example, John T. Matthews thinks that "Faulkner's *complicated* resistance to modernity may be seen in 'The Tall Men,' one of Faulkner's bluntest stories about the federal government's latest invasion of the South" ("Faulkner's Stories" 227), and Robert H. Brinkmeyer, Jr. describes it as "a simplistic tract attacking big government and extolling the virtues of the simple folk" (310). See Faulkner's *Selected Letters* for his correspondence with Robert K. Haas about writing "The Tall Men" to "finish paying the back income tax" (139).
14 Blotner reports that Faulkner worked on "Go Down, Moses" on July 19, 1940 (*A Biography* [1984] 421), and wrote "The Tall Men" in early 1941 (427).
15 Faulkner later changes the spelling to "Molly," and I change my spelling to remain consistent with Faulkner's usage.

Chapter Three

1 As Thomas Carmichael notes, the lines that Stevens misquotes should read as follows: "The scattered tea goes with the leaves. / And simply crossed her yellow sleeves; / And every day a sunset dies" (24).
2 Carmichael believes Stevens "appears to understand" how "his own observations run contrary to the import of Barnes's poem which is preoccupied with temporality and loss" (24).
3 See Robert W. Hamblin's entries for "Dixiecrat" and "*Intruder in the Dust*" in *A William Faulkner Encyclopedia* for concise discussions of the party and its influence on the novel.
4 Davis similarly suggests that *Go Down, Moses* might serve as both "Faulkner's accommodation to and contestation of cultural rituals and ideologies that ultimately as a white racial southern male subject he cannot dissemble" (197).

Chapter Four

1 See, for example, John F. Jebb's dissertation (287) and Ladd's "Philosophers and Other Gynecologists." Ladd thinks Polk "Stevens's harshest critic" and believes other scholars "are less inclined to condemn Stevens" (489-90).
2 Kelly Lynch Reames also provides compelling evidence that Temple "resents the appropriation of her story by the man who coerced her into telling it" (35), and Diane Roberts similarly feels that Temple "is duped into turning her soul inside out, for her own good, according to Gavin" (221). Finally, even Millgate revises his earlier reading of *Requiem* and determines that Polk "is surely right in insisting that it is Faulkner's primary intention to enforce a radical criticism of Stevens's increasingly arid pursuit of an abstract conception of justice and truth" ("Firmament" 32-33).
3 In a reading along the lines of the first sort, Dunlap contends that by "forcing Temple into her confession, Stevens has given her hope" (152). She also gives voice to elements of the

second type of interpretation when she notes that Stevens "'sacrifices' his professional ethics for what he thinks is a nobler reason, and, in the process, his client dies. Nancy sacrifices her life to save a marriage and, in the process, kills a child. Some lack or need within both lead them to play God with human life—still, they both mean well" (155).

4 The first five stories in *Knight's Gambit* were originally published by magazines prior to the publication of *Intruder in the Dust*: "Smoke" by *Harper's* in April 1932, "Monk" by *Scribner's* in May 1937, "Hand Upon the Waters" by *The Saturday Evening Post* in November 1939, "Tomorrow" by the *Post* in 1940, and "An Error in Chemistry" by *Ellery Queen's Mystery Magazine* in 1946. For the most part, Faulkner simply used the magazine text as setting copy for the stories of the collected volume and heavily revised the title novella (see McHaney vii-x for the complete texual history). I place my consideration of *Knight's Gambit* in this chapter because I am concerned with the entire collection, and especially with the contrast between Stevens's actions in the early stories and those he takes in the revised 1948 novella. Originally published in 1949, the collection appeared after *Intruder in the Dust* (1948) and before *Requiem for a Nun* (1951).

5 Frederick R. Karl likewise writes off *Knight's Gambit* as "one of Faulkner's weakest collections of stories," a "kind of refuse bin for second-rate material, published as a volume when Faulkner had little else to show for the 1940s" (407, 660).

6 Jerome F. Klinkowitz deals most thoroughly with the theme of the outsider in Jefferson and determines, "the community-outlander theme is the heart and strength of the *Knight's Gambit* collection" (99). Irwin painstakingly traces the roots of the detective story in American fiction, and shows how Faulkner alters that formula in key ways: "It is only when Faulkner pushes the detective story to the limits of the short story form that he is able to bend it to his own artistic will" ("*Knight's Gambit*" 104).

7 Although many scholars see Stevens as a harbinger of justice, one who, as Jebb puts it, "is an undaunted servant of higher justice" (136), only one critic devotes an entire essay to this topic. In "Truth and Justice in *Knight's Gambit*," W.E. Schlepper examines Faulkner's use of the two concepts.

8 I rely here on Jebb's translation, p. 146.

9 I presume, of course, that Stevens does not go so far as to perjure himself at the inquest.

10 I preserve the single quotation marks that indicate dialogue throughout *Knight's Gambit*. Although Faulkner remains consistent on the use of single quotation marks throughout the text, there are significant variances of usage between these first five stories and the final novella, such as the atypical inclusion of apostrophes in short contractions like "can't" and "don't," resulting from the use of magazine tearsheets for the setting copy for most of the collection.

11 While Faulkner does not explicitly use the adjective "doglike," he establishes a very similar relationship. The depth of Joe's devotion becomes quite apparent when, for example, he lies near wherever Lonnie sleeps so as to "hear him who was brother and father both, breathing. It was his one sound out of all the voiceless earth. He was infallibly aware of it" (KG 67).

12 In one such example, Skei writes that Stevens "not only shows greater understanding than ever before; he also tries to teach Chick a moral lesson" ("Detection" 85).

13 He wrote of the matter to Harold Ober, "What a commentary. In France, I am the father of a literary movement. In Europe I am considered the best modern American and among the first of all writers. In America, I eke out a hack's motion picture wages by winning second prize in a manufactured mystery story contest" (SL 217-218).

14 For example, Skei writes, "The point of the story lies somewhere else, though. Signor Canova [Flint] might easily have slipped away from detection and from Yoknapatawpha if he had not felt the need to play a final act as illusionist. His vanity is indeed what reveals

• NOTES • 101

his terrible acts, and Stevens interprets this as a 'supreme contempt for mankind'" ("Detection" 87).

15 Faulkner sets up this connection in "Hand" when he writes that the townspeople know Stevens, "voting for him year after year and calling him by his given name even though they did not quite understand him, just as they did not understand the Harvard Phi Beta Kappa key on his watch chain" (*KG* 67).

16 Stevens similarly structures Temple's confession to the governor as a game when he interjects himself into her narrative, remarking "Wait. Let me play too" (*RN* 558), and "Oh yes, I'm still playing" (560).

17 In *The Town*, Chick Mallison observes that while Stevens served as "a stretcher-bearer with the German army" for five months, he later took an "appointment as a Y.M.C.A. secretary, to go back to France with the first American troops" (91-92). However, this circumstance seems to result from Faulkner's failure to remember that in *Knight's Gambit*, Stevens actually served "three years as a stretcher-bearer in the French army" (147). In such a capacity, Stevens would have remained on the periphery of battle but would likely have seen far more of the "tunnel of blood and excrement and fear" than he would have as a Y. M. C. A. secretary.

18 Schlepper and Irwin both identify Raymond Chandler as a possible source (373, "*Knight's Gambit*" 106), though to very different ends than mine.

Chapter Five

1 Although Marta Powell Harley's reading does not stand alone, scholars tend to, as Taylor Hagood points out, "address more generally chivalric elements in [Faulkner's] work rather than to explicate Faulkner's specific uses of Arthurian material" (153). In addition to Hagood's work, see Michael N. Salda's "William Faulkner's Arthurian Tale: *Mayday*" for another insightful exploration of Faulkner's use of the legend. Salda by far offers the most comprehensive analysis of *Mayday* as he carefully evaluates it in light of existing criticism and biographical and textual influences. In focusing on *Sir Gawain*, though, I do not mean to imply that the Gawain legend exists as an isolated source.

2 Harley notes that Faulkner might have read Jessie L. Weston's popular prose version of *Sir Gawain and the Green Knight*, and draws textual similarities between it and "The Bear" (112). I attempted to ascertain which translation Faulkner would have most likely relied upon but met with little success. Although Blotner's *William Faulkner's Library: A Catalogue* does not list the Gawain story as a separate text, it appears in an anthology titled *Literary Types and Themes* (146-65). The text, however, bears a copyright date of 1960, only two years before Faulkner's death in the summer of 1962. It also seems likely that Faulkner received it as a courtesy from the publisher because it reprints both "The Bear" (76-83) and "Old Man" (184-222). Faulkner's library did contain a copy of *Bulfinch's Mythology: The Age of Fable, The Age of Chivalry, Legends of Charlemagne* which contains several Arthurian legends, including ones concerning Gawain, but not the Green Knight tale. In addition to Weston's version, Faulkner might have accessed any number of translations, including ones by Theodore Howard Banks, Jr., Sir Israel Gollancz et al., or J.R.R. Tolkien and E.V. Gordon's, all of which the University of Mississippi library currently holds. I work from Tolkien and Gordon's text because I could establish two possible points at which Faulkner might have encountered versions of it; John Cloy, bibliographer for the humanities at the University of Mississippi, confirmed that the library acquired its 1930 corrected impression of the text on November 2, 1944, and the British edition debuted in 1925, the year that

Faulkner traveled through Europe and most likely began to conceive of his own Arthurian tale, *Mayday*. On September 13, 1925, Faulkner wrote home to his mother, mentioning "a sort of fairy tale that has been buzzing in my head." Blotner speculates that the "fairy tale" might have become *Mayday*, which Faulkner probably completed during the spring or summer of 1926 (SL 22). For clarity's sake, I refer to Tolkien's first American translation in hopes that, as Tolkien wrote of his translation of *Pearl*, "this version may possibly be acceptable even to those who already know the original, and possess editions with all their apparatus" (7). Tolkien's son, Christopher Tolkien, who collected his father's translations and saw to their posthumous publication, writes in the volume's introduction that line numbers are missing from *Sir Gawain* "in accordance with my father's wishes" (24). I have added them for ease of reference, and all subsequent references to the volume are parenthetical and arranged according to Tolkien's division of *Sir Gawain* by fitt, stanza, and line. By no means do I claim that Faulkner definitely read Tolkien and Gordon's version, only that my use of this translation seems the most logical choice given the limited information available.

3   Gowan Stevens's name constitutes another derivative, though he shares little else with the Gawain figure. In *Sanctuary*, Gowan functions as another of Faulkner's knights, with his chivalric drunken cries regarding Temple Drake's plight: "'Got proteck. . . . . . .' Gowan muttered '. . . .girl. 'Ginia gem. . . . . . . gemman got proteck. . . . . . .'" (229). Later, in *Requiem for a Nun*, Gowan claims that this same sense of honor compelled him to marry Temple even after Popeye held her for a month in Miss Reba's Memphis whorehouse; Gowan thinks, "Marrying her was purest Old Virginia" (521).

4   It seems crucial to acknowledge some potential complications in my choice of *Mayday* and the last two books of the trilogy as thematic markers in this chapter for the near-beginning and near-end of Faulkner's career. First, Faulkner's preface to *The Mansion* describes the last novel of the Snopes trilogy as "the final chapter of, and the summation of, a work conceived and begun in 1925" (331). However, as Polk points out of the Snopes material in "Idealism in *The Mansion*," the "final product differs from what he [Faulkner] would have written if he had completed his Snopes work in the mid-twenties or in the early 1940s" (112). Theresa M. Towner similarly observes in *Faulkner on the Color Line: The Later Novels*, "In writing his Snopes stories and novels, then, he fundamentally rewrote and reviewed his original vision of that ubiquitous family and its patriarch" (74).

5   Since I deal with specific, isolated manifestations of idealism in Faulkner's fiction, I want to acknowledge the larger complexity of the topic. As Blotner points out in "Continuity and Change in Faulkner's Life and Art," the range of idealism in Faulkner's fiction "is so broad as to elude easy definition" (17). In fact, Bleikasten contends that "most, if not all of Faulkner's novels, from *Flags in the Dust* to *A Fable*, are at once reflections of and reflections on idealism" (37-38).

6   Wisdom permitted only a handful of scholars to study it, and it did not become accessible until he donated it to Tulane University; Tulane and Notre Dame University Press quickly published a limited facsimile issue of the text including twenty-five presentation copies and 125 for sale, most of which, as Salda observes, "disappeared into private hands" (349). It later became widely available with the publication of a trade edition in 1980, yet very few Faulknerians have written seriously about it. Faulkner dated the original January 27, 1926. See Salda's fourth footnote and first appendix for discussions of the bibliographic confusion surrounding the discrepancy between *Mayday*'s copyright and publication dates (365, 369-73).

7   Carvel Collins's introductory essay that accompanies the facsimile and trade editions of *Mayday* addresses all of these concerns. Brooks's 1977 essay, "The Image of Helen Baird in Faulkner's Early Poetry and Fiction," connects *Mayday* to Faulkner's own failed romances

with Estelle Oldham and Helen Baird and articulates the textual connection between Faulkner's narrative and James Branch Cabell's *Jurgen*. Gail Moore Morrison's "Time, Tide, and Twilight: *Mayday* and Faulkner's Quest Toward *The Sound and the Fury*" (1978) likewise analyzes source material and shows how the text looks ahead to *The Sound and the Fury*. James G. Watson's "Literary Self-Criticism: Faulkner in Fiction on Fiction" (1981-82) contains a biographical reading of the text as parody and detailed explanations of the accompanying sketches and watercolor illustrations. Harley's essay in *American Notes and Queries* (1982-83) mentions the connection between *Mayday* and *Sir Gawain and the Green Knight*. Calvin S. Brown's 1980 review essay, "Faulkner, Criticism, and High Fashion," notes the publication of *Mayday* as a trade edition and comments briefly upon the text. Philip Cohen's 1984 "Faulkner's Players and his Pawns" examines *Mayday*'s use of the metaphor of a "mysterious Player moving pieces on a cosmic chessboard" and connects it to Cabell's *Jurgen* (16), and Cohen's 1986 essay, "Horace Benbow and Faulkner's Other Early Failed Idealists," examines Galwyn and other early characters as precursors to Faulkner's later disillusioned Prufrockian intellectuals. Salda considers the text at length in his "William Faulkner's Arthurian Tale: *Mayday*" (1994); this essay reads the narrative closely, outlines its history and sources, and catalogues the existing criticism. Since the publication of Salda's essay, Shigeru Hanaoka has also approached *Mayday* as Faulkner's examination of romance in an Arthurian setting in "On *Mayday*."

8   Christopher Dean also says of Gawain, "On the one hand, he has been seen favorably as an ideal warrior of almost saint-like purity and as a Christ figure, on the other, he has been regarded unfavorably as a rash, passionate soldier, the epitome of reckless folly serving as a warning to all headstrong men who turn their backs on reason" (115). Dean could easily describe not only Gawain but also Stevens, further highlighting a basic similarity in their characters.

9   Harley notes that, as in *Sir Gawain and the Green Knight*, Stevens's "dealings with Eula offer a series of three's" (111).

10 Stevens does not include himself in this number because, as Ratliff points out, when Eula asked Stevens to marry Linda, "it was like she had said right out in public that he [Stevens] wouldn't a had no hope [of having a relationship with Eula] even if Manfred de Spain hadn't never laid eyes on her" (457).

11 Stevens's frequent, premature misinterpretations of various situations also support such a reading. For example, in *The Town*, Stevens points out that people generally fail to search for the true character behind the superficially projected personae of others; as he crosses the square, he remarks of Otis Harker, the night marshal, "he wasn't looking at me at all: he was watching me, deferent to my white hairs as a well-'raised' Mississippian should be." Ironically, this scene makes it clear that Stevens looks no deeper into Harker's character than he believes Harker does into his. When he and Harker engage in conversation and, in typical fashion, Stevens reads more into Harker's response than seems warranted, Harker calls him on it, remarking, "I dont believe I quite said that, did I?" (279-80).

12 When Eula speculates, "Maybe it's because you're a gentleman and I never knew one before," Stevens immediately replies, "So is Manfred! . . . And that other one, that first one—your child's father—" (*T* 83). Stevens's definition of these two men as gentlemen, neither of which seems "enfeebled by refinement" as Brooks suggests, indicates that Stevens defines "gentleman" more expansively than Brooks allows for. Stevens subsequently juxtaposes his inability to "even finish the fight I started myself with just one opponent" with his belief that Hoake McCarron "fought off five or six men who tried to ambush you in the buggy that night [when Eula lost her virginity]"; Stevens says that Eula's two lovers are "Both alike" but "not like me. All three gentlemen but only two were men" (84). In *The Mansion*, Ratliff describes McCarron fighting with "a wagon-spoke now in his

remaining hand . . . while Eula was standing up in the buggy with that lead-loaded buggy whip of Will's reversed in both hands like a hoe or a axe, swinging the leaded butt of it at whatever head come up next" (441), and in *The Hamlet*, one of the attackers tells basically the same story, although instead of remaining in the buggy Eula springs from it "with the reversed whip beating three of them back while her companion used the reversed pistol-butt against the wagon-spoke and the brass knuckles of the other two" (858). According to Stevens's expansive definition, it would seem that Eula may possess more of a gentleman's courage and ability than he does.

13 In one such example, Ratliff speculates that Eula "likely" called Stevens by his "first name for the first time" when she said, "Marry her [Linda], Gavin" (M 457). In *The Town*, Eula repeats that exact phrase several times, and Stevens marvels that she uses his given name when "not once had she ever called me even Mister Stevens" (291).

14 Several other critics have alluded to this possibility. Jay Watson concludes that Stevens's "reticence is undoubtedly what drives Eula to more desperate measures, for that very night she takes her life" (228). Raymond J. Wilson likewise believes that Eula sees the "necessity for suicide" after Stevens convinces her that her departure will "finish" Linda (441).

15 Faulkner gives readers good reason to doubt Chick's ability to speak impartially for "all of Jefferson" in *The Town*. From the novel's first page, Chick seems destined to become a younger, slightly more aware version of Stevens, yet still a perpetual observer who echoes the opinions of those around him, even inadvertently, in his own speech. For example, when Chick recalls how Linda's boyfriend, Matt Levitt, blows his horn repeatedly, challenging Stevens as he passes the Mallison house in much the same way that Mayor de Spain earlier opened his cut-out, Chick says that he "smelled something, caught a whiff of something for a second that even if I located it again I still wouldn't know whether I had ever smelled it before or not" (T 163). Actually, Chick could not identify the smell because he never smells anything; he merely echoes his father's caustic observation that as Matt passed, he smelled "something we haven't smelled around here" since the mayor similarly passed by long ago, probably a reference to the supposed "scent" of Gavin's fear and shame (164). In another such instance, Chick echoes Eula when he talks of Linda's future after her mother's suicide and remarks, "I know now that people really are kind, they really are" (299). Eula earlier told Stevens that the people of Jefferson might have shielded her parents from the knowledge of her affair with Manfred de Spain because "people are really kind, you know" (289). Chick seems to have heard Stevens repeat Eula's comment and adopted the sentiment as his own, likely unconsciously. This behavior, combined with Chick's penchant for taking up Ratliff's and Stevens's respective speech patterns whenever he talks to them, makes obvious that, as the "voice of Jefferson," Chick hardly records events any more objectively than Faulkner's other narrators.

16 Dawn Trouard also refers to a passage in *The Hamlet* in which Faulkner describes Eula almost as a statue using "the language of mortuary, effigy, even death mask" and points out that "Faulkner reads Eula, early in her career as Mrs. Snopes, into the tradition of waiting women, women who preside over graveyards, stilled women, who are captured into legends and male myths" (284).

17 In "Taken Men and Token Women in *Sir Gawain and the Green Knight*," Sheila Fisher suggests that the Gawain poet erases the Lady of Hautdesert from the text in a similar fashion. Fisher notes that when Gawain returns from his quest, Arthur's "court makes a magnanimous move that completes the erasure of the Lady and her meaning(s) from the girdle" when they attempt "to relieve Gawain of his apparently morbid obsession with a rather small sin" by agreeing "to wear the girdle, to take it as a collective symbol" (97).

18 This is, of course, only one source of the evolution. The would-be lover who crafted *Mayday* as a courtship gift for Helen Baird in 1926 was a very different man from the one

who composed *The Town* over thirty years later while corresponding with Jean Stein about the novel (SL 391, 393, 399, 402) . Oddly enough, when Stein visited Mississippi just before Faulkner began writing *The Town*, they unexpectedly encountered Baird; Blotner writes of the meeting: "Now the cold autumn beach was deserted, except for one other figure. As they approached, he [Faulkner] saw that it was Helen Baird Lyman. Widowed and ill, she had nonetheless retained her old tartness. Later, when she told Ann Farnsworth that she had met Bill Faulkner on the beach, she said, 'He had some young girl with him. But you have to expect that'" (Blotner, *A Biography* [1984] 615-16).

19   This political material, though, literally intruded upon the novel's composition in that drafts of essays, speeches, and letters to different newspapers and various individuals appear on the versos of the early typescripts for *The Town* and *The Mansion*. For a discussion of these materials, see Eileen Gregory.

20   In the next sentence, Urgo adds that he feels such assertions "are wholly misleading."

21   In "The Roster, the Chronicle, and the Critic " Towner says of such perceptions, "nearly every . . . Faulkner scholar upon learning this fact has uttered a dismissive comment on that fiction; but every one who has done so also followed such a comment with some disclaimer for a particular later novel. By this time, I have now heard the later fiction dismissed with the exceptions of every one of the later novels, which I take as anecdotal evidence for my point of view and not just the wish of Faulkner scholars to be polite in conversation" (4-5).

Chapter Six

1   The loyalty the nameless black man expresses for Linda when Mink suggests "Likely she can hear ever bit as good as you and me" indicates that Linda's efforts have not been completely in vain. Of course, Mink actually fishes for information here as he tries to discover whether Linda might actually hear the gunshot when he kills Flem, but the man warns Mink, "If I was you, I dont believe I would dispute it. Or leastways I would be careful who I disputed it to." He adds, "The Lord touched her, like He touches a heap of folks better than you, better than me" (M 690). Mink later thinks with irritation, "that nigger jest yestiddy evening. . . got almost impident, durn nigh called a white man a liar to his face the least suh-jestion I made that maybe she was fooling folks" (701-02), but Mink seems to sense something of the power that the man alludes to when Linda finds him standing over Flem's body: "for an instant he thought *So she could hear all the time* before he knew better: she didn't need to hear; it was the same power brought her here to catch him that by merely pointing her finger at him could blast, annihilate, vaporise him where he stood" (703).

2   At the thirty-third annual Faulkner and Yoknapatawpha Conference exploring "Global Faulkner," Manuel Broncano offered another possible motivation by reading Linda's involvement in the Spanish War as "parallel to the war within the Snopes family, Mink versus Flem, the dispossessed versus the capitalist, honor versus shameless ambition." Broncano believes that in this war, "Linda takes sides with Mink, as she sides with the Republican cause, and hers is a fight for justice" that ends with her restoring "the de Spain family to its legitimate estate, the mansion that gives title to the novel" (110). While I am not sure that such a heroic reading of Mink embodies Faulkner's view, it certainly seems representative of Linda's.

3   I do not intend, however, to denigrate the number of critical readings that highlight what Hee Kang refers to as Linda's "feminine autonomy." Kang notes that Linda acts out of

"rage against the father" (25) in addition to her "growth in consciousness and her courage to act" (Fulton 427), and adds that Linda's "revenge reveals her creative power to interpret critically the world surrounding her, a birth of a new feminine consciousness which negates the Father's law. Charles informs us that, unlike Eula and young Linda, the returned, mature Linda is no longer the object of Flem's transaction for his economic and political rise" (Kang 25). It is significant that this new consciousness includes learning to use Flem's and Stevens's own methods against them. Faulkner points to the similarities between Flem's and Stevens's tactics when Chick describes how they combine forces to put Montgomery Ward's "Atelier Monty" out of business: "that's when Uncle Gavin found out that he and Mr Snopes were looking at exactly the same thing: they were just standing in different places" (148).

4 For example, Eula knows of Linda's strong attachment to Flem, despite their difficulties. As Eula says, "you—a girl anyway—dont really hate your father no matter how much you think you do or should or should want to" (T 282). Moreover, Ratliff trusts Eula enough to tell her about his Russian ancestry and his given name, Vladimir Kyrilytch Ratcliffe (283). Eula also tells Stevens that Flem "cant" have sex. "He's—what's the word? impotent. He's always been. Maybe that's why, one of the reasons You see? You've got to be careful or you'll have to pity him. You'll have to. He couldn't bear that, and it's no use to hurt people if you dont get anything for it. Because he couldn't bear being pitied" (291). While Eula's remark may reveal rare, sensitive insight into Flem's psyche, it may have more to do with her awareness of Stevens's distaste for Flem than with Flem's sexual capabilities. Much earlier in the novel, after Stevens refuses Eula's offer of sex, Stevens convinces himself, "oh yes, I knew now: Snopes himself was impotent. I even said it [to Eula]." While Stevens does not *quite* say it, he does speak of Hoake McCarron as one of her two lovers, the "only other one besides Manfred" (83). In fact, this comment could constitute yet another of Stevens's lies to himself. In chapter eight of *The Town*, he reveals that he always thinks of Eula as "Eula Varner. Never Eula Snopes even though I had—had had to—watched them [Eula and Flem] in bed together" (117). This certainly does not mean that Stevens saw them having sex, and Stevens could easily exaggerate, but Faulkner lends credence to the possibility when Gowan strongly suspects Stevens of spying, so much so that he tries for a week to catch Stevens in the ditch behind Snopes's house. However, as Chick notes, "if Uncle Gavin was hid somewhere in that ditch too, Gowan never caught him" (46).

5 Although Flem thinks he has "bought" Eula and "cashed in" on her death, readers really have no way of knowing why Eula committed suicide. The novel fails to substantiate either Stevens's assertion that Eula killed herself to "leave her child a mere suicide for a mother instead of a whore," or Ratliff's speculation that she did it because "she was bored" (T 299, 315). Holli G. Levitsky points out that Ratliff's comment ironically compares "Eula's self-wrought death to Emma Bovary's escape from the ennui and insatiate desires of her stifling bourgeois existence" (32). *The Mansion*, however, similarly describes young Bayard Sartoris's "boredom" upon returning from World War I, and suggests that Eula, like Bayard, might suffer from self-destructive tendencies resulting from some form of traumatic stress. Charles describes how Bayard effectively commits suicide as he tries to "relieve his boredom by seeing how much faster he could make something travel than he could invent a destination for; this time another aeroplane: a new experimental type at the Dayton testing field: only this one fooled him by shedding all four of its wings in midair" (501).

6 Before Linda asks Stevens to help her secure Mink's pardon, the narrator observes that Stevens "had no idea what Linda wanted either" (M 658). While it would seem that Stevens hasn't a clue about what Linda will ask of him, he goes on to reveal that he hasn't a clue about Linda, period, when he extrapolates, "*Because women are wonderful: it doesn't*

really matter what they want or if they themselves even know what it is they think they want" (658). It later becomes clear that Linda knows exactly what she wants, Mink's release, as she skillfully manipulates Stevens into helping her secure it.

7   Although a blank space about five ems long did appear in the first edition, Polk assured me in an e-mail sent in June of 2006 that it was the result of an editorial decision at Random House, perhaps made with Faulkner's collaboration and even approval. No extra spacing appears in the typescript or in the corrected Library of America text.

8   Linda's wish for Stevens to marry another could also echo Guinevere's plea in *Le Morte D'Arthur* that, after the fall of Camelot, Launcelot leave her in the nunnery and "go to thy realm, and there take thee a wife, and live with her with joy and bliss" (930).

9   To facilitate such an arrangement, Stevens apparently even enters into a marriage that allows him to continue thinking of himself in such a fashion. In *The Town* Chick describes Stevens's future wife, Melisandre Backus Harriss, as a woman "whose terrible power was that defenselessness and helplessness which conferred knighthood on any man who came within range, before he had a chance to turn and flee" (157).

10 The entry for Pyramus and Thisbe in the edition of *Bulfinch's Mythology* from Faulkner's library begins, "Pyramus was the handsomest youth, and Thisbe the fairest maiden, in all Babylonia, where Semiramis reigned" (24).

11 At the 2006 Faulkner and Yoknapatawpha Conference, Matthews carefully analyzed the relationship between Linda and Stevens as he spoke to the influence Stevens holds over her future with his campaign to "emancipate her": "Stevens undertakes Linda's informal education during these sessions, tutoring her in the poets, telling her about northern colleges, and mostly urging her to get out of Jefferson and leave everything Snopes behind. Stevens directs her toward New York City, not as the classic destination for materializing the American dream, but as the place where she can discover oppositional culture. Linda's escape to Greenwich Village yields her a Jewish lover, a communist sculptor committed to radical politics and experimental aesthetics. Already signaled by Gavin's refusal to touch his Coca-Cola, Linda's liberation constitutes a different kind of freedom; it repudiates 'the free Snopes world' of money-making and consumption. She bids to emancipate herself from false norms of behavior attached to national origin, region, class, family, race, gender, marital relation—norms fetishized by Cold War America, but discredited here as functioning primarily to rationalize power-holding" ("Many Mansions" 15). I would suggest that Linda also acts to emancipate herself from Stevens's paternalism as she leaves Jefferson for "New York as soon as the funeral was over" (M 708).

12 Stevens's penchant for such pursuits seems well-known indeed in that even Eef Bishop knows of it. He describes Stevens's fears for Flem's life as "just another of Lawyer Stevens's nightmares" (M 697).

13 Although Faulkner does not name Gawain and Ragnelle's story specifically, or even the similar tale told by Chaucer's Wife of Bath, it seems a likely source given Stevens's close connection to the Gawain figure, its similarity to the Gawain tale, and its central concern with feminine autonomy. In brief, Sir Gromer challenges King Arthur to discover within one year what women most desire, or he must pay with his life. Gromer's sister, the most unattractive Lady Ragnelle, provides the answer Arthur seeks (women most desire sovereignty) on the condition that Sir Gawain will marry her. Gawain essentially takes on Arthur's challenge again as he did with the Green Knight, agreeing to marry Ragnelle to save his king. After the ceremony, Ragnelle turns into the most beautiful woman Gawain has ever seen because Gawain's willingly wedding her has weakened the curse she was under. However, Ragnelle tells Gawain that she can only appear beautiful for half the day; she asks him to choose whether he would prefer her to appear beautiful during the day when they are with others or at night, when they are alone. Gawain leaves the choice to

her, granting her the sovereignty that she told Arthur that women most desire, and this answer lifts the spell completely, allowing her to retain her beauty all day long. Ragnelle, like Linda, has already selected the knight she wishes to do her bidding and Gawain, like Stevens, sacrifices himself for what he views as a worthy cause.

Chapter Seven

1. Olga W. Vickery identifies Lucius, Boon, and Ned as knights and writes that as they assume their roles as such "the customary social definition of their relationship is soon forgotten. As knights they are peers, and indeed all three of them can claim to be of noble birth." Lucius and Ned, of course, descend from old Yoknapatawpha families, and Boon identifies himself as "a lineal royal descendant of old Issetibbeha himself" (233).
2. Faulkner wrote to Albert Erskine, "The title for what they are doing would be The Stealers. The title I have now is The Reavers." Faulkner added, "there is an old Scottish spelling which I like better: The Rievers (maybe *Reivers*)"; Faulkner preferred the alternate spelling because reavers "sounds too peaceful, bucolic: too much like Weavers" (SL 456).
3. I would argue, however, that Corrie has just as much to do with orchestrating that "conventional happy ending," and that the ending may turn out to be less idyllic than we are led to believe given Boon's casual attitude towards his physical abuse of Corrie: "what better sign than a black eye or a cut mouf can a woman want from a man that he got her on his mind?" (R 937).
4. Brooks observed early on, "Many of Faulkner's characters exalt the horse and chivalry" and noted that "Faulkner, as early as *Sartoris*, pays his respect to the homely mule, and it is no accident that some of the characters he most admires understand the mule and partake of his intelligence, his common sense, and his stubborn patience" (*William Faulkner* 363).

Works Cited

Works by Faulkner

Faulkner, William. *Absalom, Absalom!* 1936. *William Faulkner: Novels 1936-1940.* Ed. Joseph Blotner and Noel Polk. New York: Library of America, 1990. 1-315.
——. *Collected Stories of William Faulkner.* 1934. Vintage international ed. New York: Random House, 1995.
——. *Essays, Speeches, and Public Letters.* Ed. James B. Meriwether. New York: Random House, 1965.
——. *Faulkner in the University: Class Conferences at the University of Virginia 1957-1958.* Ed. Frederick L. Gwynn and Joseph L. Blotner. Charlottesville: U of Virginia P, 1959.
——. *Faulkner at West Point.* Ed. Joseph L. Fant and Robert Ashely. New York: Random House, 1964.
——. *Flags in the Dust.* 1973. *William Faulkner: Novels 1926-1929.* Ed. Joseph Blotner and Noel Polk. New York: Library of America, 2006. 541-875.
——. *The Hamlet. William Faulkner: Novels 1936-1940.* Ed. Joseph Blotner and Noel Polk. New York: Library of America, 1990. 727-1075.
——. *Intruder in the Dust.* 1948. *William Faulkner: Novels 1942-1954.* Ed. Joseph Blotner and Noel Polk. New York: Library of America, 1994. 283-470.
——. *Knight's Gambit.* New York: Random House, 1949.
——. *Lion in the Garden: Interviews with William Faulkner 1926-1962.* Ed. James B. Meriwether and Michael Millgate. New York: Random House, 1968.
——. *The Mansion.* 1959. *William Faulkner: Novels 1957-1962.* Ed. Joseph Blotner and Noel Polk. New York: Library of America, 1999. 327-721.
——. *Mayday.* 1926. Ed. Carvel Collins. Notre Dame: U of Notre Dame P, 1976.
——. *The Reivers: A Reminiscence.* 1962. *Novels 1957-1962.* Ed. Joseph Blotner and Noel Polk. New York: Library of America, 1999. 723-971.
——. *Requiem for a Nun.* 1951. *William Faulkner: Novels 1942-1954.* Ed. Joseph Blotner and Noel Polk. New York: Library of America, 1994. 471-664.
——. "Rose of Lebanon." *Oxford American.* May-June 1995. 54-73.
——. *Sanctuary.* 1931. *William Faulkner: Novels 1930-1935.* Ed. Joseph Blotner and Noel Polk. New York: Library of America, 1985. 179-398.
——. *Selected Letters of William Faulkner.* Ed. Joseph Blotner. New York: Random House, 1977.
——. *The Town.* 1957. *William Faulkner: Novels 1957-62.* Ed. Joseph Blotner and Noel Polk. New York: Library of America, 1999. 1-326.
——. *Uncollected Stories of William Faulkner.* 1979. Ed. Joseph Blotner. Vintage international ed. New York: Random House, 1997.
——. *William Faulkner Manuscripts 18*: Knight's Gambit. Ed. Thomas L. McHaney. New York: Garland, 1987.

Works by Others

Beck, Warren. *Man in Motion: Faulkner's Trilogy.* Madison: U of Wisconsin P, 1961.
Betts, Doris. "Many Souths and Broadening Scale: A Changing Southern Literature." *The Future South: A Historical Perspective for the Twenty-first Century.* Ed. Joe P. Dunn and Howard L. Preston. Urbana: U of Illinois P, 1991. 158-87.
Bleikasten, André. "For / Against an Ideological Reading of Faulkner's Novels." *Faulkner and Idealism: Perspectives from Paris.* Ed. Michel Gresset and Patrick Samway, S.J. Jackson: UP of Mississippi, 1983. 27-50.
Blotner, Joseph. "Continuity and Change in Faulkner's Life and Art." *Faulkner and Idealism: Perspectives from Paris.* Ed. Michel Gresset and Patrick Samway, S.J. Jackson: UP of Mississippi, 1983. 15-26.
———. *Faulkner: A Biography.* 2 vols. New York: Random House, 1974. Revised, 1 vol. New York: Random House, 1984.
———. "Mr. Faulkner: Writer-In-Residence." *Virginia Quarterly Review* 77.2 (2001): 323-38.
———. *William Faulkner's Library: A Catalogue.* Charlottesville: UP of Virginia, 1964.
Brinkmeyer, Robert H., Jr. "A Fighting Faith: Faulkner, Democratic Ideology, and the World War II Home Front." *William Faulkner's Short Fiction: An International Symposium.* Ed. Hans H. Skei. Oslo: Solum Forlag, 1997. 306-15.
Broncano, Manuel. "Reading Faulkner in Spain, Reading Spain in Faulkner." *Global Faulkner: Faulkner and Yoknapatawpha, 2006.* Ed. Annette Trefzer and Ann J. Abadie. Jackson: UP of Mississippi, 2009. 99-115.
Brooks, Cleanth. "Gavin Stevens and the Chivalric Tradition." *Studies in English* 15 (1978): 19-32.
———. "The Image of Helen Baird in Faulkner's Early Poetry and Fiction." *Sewanee Review* 85.2 (1977): 218-34.
———. *William Faulkner: The Yoknapatawpha Country.* New Haven: Yale UP, 1963.
Brown, Calvin S. "Faulkner, Criticism, and High Fashion." *Sewanee Review* 88.1 (1980): 631-41.
Bulfinch, Thomas. *Bulfinch's Mythology: The Age of Fable, The Age of Chivalry, The Age of Charlemagne.* Ed. Bennett A. Cerf and Donald S. Klopfer. New York: Modern Library, 1934.
Carmichael, Thomas. "Intruder in the Text: Faulkner's Djuna Barnes." *Faulkner Journal* 14.1 (1998): 21-30.
Carothers, James B. "The Rhetoric of Faulkner's Later Fiction, and of Its Critics." *Faulkner's Discourse: An International Symposium.* Ed. Lothar Hönnighausen. Tübingen: Max Niemeyer Verlag, 1989. 263-70.
Chandler, Raymond. *The Big Sleep.* 1939. *Raymond Chandler: Stories and Early Novels.* Ed. Frank MacShane. New York: Library of America, 587-764.
Clein, Wendy. *Concepts of Chivalry in Sir Gawain and the Green Knight.* Norman, Oklahoma: Pilgrim Books, 1987.
Cobb, James C. *Away Down South: A History of Southern Identity.* New York: Oxford UP, 2005.
Cohen, Philip. "Faulkner's Player and His Pawns: The Source of a Metaphor." *American Notes & Queries* 23.1-2 (1984): 16-19.
———. "Horace Benbow and Faulkner's Other Early Failed Idealists." *South Carolina Review* 18.2 (1986): 78-92.

Collins, Carvel. Introduction. *Mayday*. Notre Dame: U of Notre Dame P, 1978. 1-41.
Davenport, F. Garvin, Jr. *The Myth of Southern History: Historical Consciousness in Twentieth Century Southern Literature*. Nashville: Vanderbilt UP, 1967.
Davis, Thadious M. *Games of Property: Law, Race, Gender, and Faulkner's* Go Down, Moses. Durham and London: Duke UP, 2003.
Dean, Christopher. "Sir Gawain in the Alliterative *Morte Arthure*." *Papers on Language and Literature* 22.2 (1986): 115-25.
Dunlap, Mary Montgomery. *The Achievement of Gavin Stevens*. Diss. U of South Carolina, 1970. Ann Arbor: UMI, 1970. 7027046.
Dussere, Erik. "The Debts of History: Southern Honor, Affirmative Action, and Faulkner's *Intruder in the Dust*." *Faulkner Journal* 17.1 (2001): 37-57.
Ferguson, James. *Faulkner's Short Fiction*. Knoxville: U of Tennessee P, 1991.
Fisher, Sheila. "Taken Men and Token Women in *Sir Gawain and the Green Knight*." *Seeking the Woman in Late Medieval and Renaissance Writings: Essays in Feminist Contextual Criticism*. Ed. Sheila Fisher and Janet E. Halley. Knoxville: U of Tennessee P, 1989. 71-105.
Flannery, M.C. and John G. Cawelti. "Gavin Stevens: Faulkner's Favorite." *ANQ* 4.1 (1991): 21-24.
Fulton, Keith Louise. "Linda Snopes Kohl: Faulkner's Radical Woman." *Modern Fiction Studies* 34.3 (1988): 425-36.
Garrett, George. Introduction. *Snopes*: The Hamlet, The Town, The Mansion. By William Faulkner. New York: Modern Library, 1994. vii-xiii.
Gregory, Eileen. "Faulkner's Typescripts of *The Town*." *Mississippi Quarterly* 26.3 (1973): 361-86.
Hagood, Taylor. *Faulkner's Imperialism: Space, Place, and the Materiality of Myth*. Baton Rouge: Louisiana State University Press, 2008..
Hamblin, Robet W. "Dixiecrat." *A William Faulkner Encyclopedia*. Ed. Robert W. Hamblin and Charles A. Peek. Westport: Greenwood Press, 103-04.
———. "Intruder in the Dust." *A William Faulkner Encyclopedia*. Ed. Robert W. Hamblin and Charles A. Peek. Westport: Greenwood Press, 1999. 199-201.
Hanaoka, Shigeru. "On *Mayday*." *Kwansei Gakuin Daigaku Keizaigakubu Ronshu* (1995): 63-71.
Harley, Marta Powell. "Faulkner's Medievalism and *Sir Gawain and the Green Knight*." *American Notes & Queries* 21.7-8 (1983): 111-14.
Hönnighausen, Lothar. *Faulkner: Masks and Metaphors*. Jackson: UP of Mississippi, 1997.
Howe, Irving. *William Faulkner: A Critical Study*. 1952. 4th ed. Chicago: Dee, 1991.
Irwin, John T. "Horace Benbow and the Myth of Narcissa." *American Literature* 64.3 (1992): 543-66.
———. "*Knight's Gambit*: Poe, Faulkner, and the Tradition of the Detective Story." *Arizona Quarterly* 46.4 (1990): 95-116.
Jebb, John F. *The Law, Justice, and Faulkner's Gavin Stevens*. Diss. U of Delaware, 1990. Ann Arbor: UMI, 1991. 9109936.
Kang, Hee. "A New Configuration of Faulkner's Feminine: Linda Snopes Kohl in *The Mansion*." *Faulkner Journal* 8.1 (1992): 21-41.
Karaganis, Joe. "Negotiating the National Voice in Faulkner's Late Work." *Arizona Quarterly* 54.4 (1998): 53-81.
Karl, Frederick R. *William Faulkner: American Writer*. New York: Weidenfeld and Nicolson, 1989.
Kartiganer, Donald. Introduction. "Rose of Lebanon." *Oxford American*. May-June 1995. 51-53.
King James Bible. 24 October 2006 <http://etext.lib.virginia.edu/kjv.browse html>.
Klinkowitz, Jerome F. "The Thematic Unity of *Knight's Gambit*." *Critique* 11.2 (1969): 81-100.
Kulseth, Leonard I. "Cincinnatus Among the Snopeses: The Role of Gavin Stevens." *Ball State University Forum* 10.1 (1969): 28-34.

Ladd, Barbara. "'Philosophers and Other Gynecologists': Women and the Polity in *Requiem for a Nun*." *Mississippi Quarterly* 52.3 (1999): 483-501.
Levitsky, Holli G. "Suicide and Sex: The Cost of Desire (is Death)." *Southern Quarterly* 41.1 (2002): 29-38.
Longley, John Lewis, Jr. *The Tragic Mask: A Study of Faulkner's Heroes*. Chapel Hill: U of North Carolina P, 1963.
Malory, Sir Thomas. *Le Morte D'Arthur*. New York: Modern Library, 1999.
Marx, Charles A. and Thomas E. Payne. "Chapter Nine: The Criminal Justice System in Mississippi." *Politics in Mississippi*, 2nd ed. Ed. Joseph B. Parker. Salem, Wisconsin: Sheffield, 2001. 181-99.
Matthews, John T. "Faulkner's Stories and New Deal Interference." *William Faulkner's Short Fiction: An International Symposium*. Ed. Hans H. Skei.Oslo: Solum Forlag, 1997. 222-29.
———. "Many Mansions: Faulkner's Cold War Conflicts." *Global Faulkner: Faulkner and Yoknapatawpha, 2006*. Ed. Annette Trefzer and Ann J. Abadie. Jackson: UP of Mississippi, 2009. 3-23.
McHaney, Thomas L. Introduction. *William Faulkner Manuscripts 18: Knight's Gambit*. Ed. Thomas L. McHaney. New York: Garland, 1987.
McMillen, Neil R. and Noel Polk. "Faulkner on Lynching." *Faulkner Journal* 7.1 (1992): 3-14.
McNamee, Maurice B., James E. Cronin, and Joseph A. Rogers, eds. *Literary Types and Themes*. New York: Holt, Rinehart, and Winston, 1960.
Meats, Stephen E. "Who Killed Joanna Burden?" *Mississippi Quarterly* 24.3 (1971): 271-77.
Meindl, Dieter. "'Rose of Lebanon' and the Faulkner Canon." *Amerikastudien* 42.2 (1997): 583-90.
Meriwether, James B. *The Literary Career of William Faulkner: A Bibliographical Study*. Princeton: Princeton University Library, 1961.
Millgate, Michael. *The Achievement of William Faulkner*. New York: Random House, 1966.
———. "'The Firmament of Man's History': Faulkner's Treatment of the Past." *Mississippi Quarterly* 25 (Spring supplement, 1972): 25-35.
Milum, Richard A. *The Cavalier Spirit in Faulkner's Fiction*. Diss. Indiana University, 1972. Ann Arbor: UMI, 1973.
Monaghan, David M. "Faulkner's Relationship to Gavin Stevens in *Intruder in the Dust*." *Dalhousie Review* 52 (1972): 449-57.
Moreland, Richard C. "Faulkner's Continuing Education: From Self-Reflection to Embarrassment." *Faulkner at 100: Retrospect and Prospect: Faulkner and Yoknapatawpha, 1997*. Ed. Donald M. Kartiganer and Ann J. Abadie. Jackson: UP of Mississippi, 2000. 60-69.
———. *Faulkner's Modernism Under Revision*. Diss. U of California, Berkley, 1987. Ann Arbor: UMI, 1987. 8726306.
Morrison, Gail Moore. "'Time, Tide, and Twilight': *Mayday* and Faulkner's Quest Toward *The Sound and the Fury*." *Mississippi Quarterly* 31.3 (1978): 337-57.
Norris, Nancy. "*The Hamlet, The Town*, and *The Mansion*: A Psychological Reading of the Snopes Trilogy." *Mosaic* 7.1 (1973): 213-35. Peckham, Morse. "The Place of Sex in the Work of William Faulkner." *Studies in the Twentieth Century* 14 (1974): 1-20.
Polk, Noel. *Children of the Dark House: Text and Context in Faulkner*. Jackson: UP of Mississippi, 1996.
———. E-mail to the author. 5 June 2006.
———. "Faulkner and Crime Fiction." *Publications of the Arkansas Philological Association* 29.1 (2003): 1-26.
———. *Faulkner's Requiem for a Nun: A Critical Study*. Bloomington: Indiana UP, 1981.
———. "Idealism in *The Mansion*." *Faulkner and Idealism: Perspectives from Paris*. Ed. Michel Gresset and Patrick Samway, S.J. Jackson: UP of Mississippi, 1983. 112-26.

———. "'Polysyllabic and Verbless Patriotic Nonsense': Faulkner at Midcentury—His and Ours." *Faulkner and Ideology: Faulkner and Yoknapatawpha, 1992*. Ed. Donald M. Kartiganer and Ann J. Abadie. Jackson: UP of Mississippi, 1995. 297-327.
Reames, Kelly Lynch. "'All That Matters Is That I Wrote the Letters': Discourse, Discipline, and Difference in *Requiem for a Nun*." *Faulkner Journal* 14.1 (1998): 31-52.
Roberts, Diane. *Faulkner and Southern Womanhood*. Athens: U of Georgia P, 1994.
Rubin, Louis D., Jr. "The Dixie Special: William Faulkner and the Southern Literary Renascence." *Faulkner and the Southern Renaissance: Faulkner and Yoknapatawpha, 1981*. Ed. Doreen Fowler and Ann J. Abadie. Jackson: UP of Mississippi, 1982. 63-92.
Salda, Michael N. "William Faulkner's Arthurian Tale: *Mayday*." *Arthuriana* 4.4 (1994): 348-75.
Samway, Patrick, S.J. "Gavin Stevens as Uncle-Creator in *Knight's Gambit*." *Faulkner and Idealism: Perspectives from Paris*. Ed. Michel Gresset and Patrick Samway, S.J. Jackson: UP of Mississippi, 1983. 144-63.
———. Introduction. *Intruder in the Dust: A Concordance to the Novel*. Ed. Noel Polk. Ann Arbor, Michigan. Faulkner Concordance Advisory Board, 1983. ix-xi.
Sayre, Robert Woods. "Artistic Self-Theft as Obsession and Creative Transformation: The 'Memphis' Stories and Beyond." *Faulkner Journal* 13.1-2 (1997-98): 37-55.
Schlepper, W.E. "Truth and Justice in *Knight's Gambit*." *Mississippi Quarterly* 37.3 (1984): 365-75.
Sir Gawain and the Green Knight. Trans. Theodore Howard Banks, Jr. New York: F.S. Crofts, 1929.
Sir Gawain and the Green Knight. Trans. Sir Israel Gollancz. London: Oxford UP, 1940.
Sir Gawain and the Green Knight. Trans. J.R.R. Tolkien and E.V. Gordon. Corrected impression. Oxford: Clarendon Press, 1930.
Sir Gawain and the Green Knight, Pearl, and Sir Orfeo. 1st American ed. Trans. J.R.R. Tolkien. Boston: Houghton Mifflin, 1975.
Sir Gawain and the Green Knight: A Middle-English Arthurian Romance Retold in Modern Prose. Trans. Jessie L. Weston. New York: New Amsterdam Book Company, 1903.
Skei, Hans H. "Faulkner's *Knight's Gambit*: Detection and Ingenuity." *Notes on Mississippi Writers* 13.2 (1981): 79-93.
———. *William Faulkner: The Novelist as Short Story Writer*. Oslo: Universitetsforlaget, 1985.
Stroble, Woodrow. "Flem Snopes: A Crazed Mirror." *Faulkner: The Unappeased Imagination: A Collection of Critical Essays*. Ed. Glenn O. Carey. New York: Whitston, 1980. 195-212.
Tangum, Marion. "Gavin Stevens." *A William Faulkner Encyclopedia*. Ed. Robert W. Hamblin and Charles A. Peek. Westport, Connecticut: Greenwood, 1999. 382-83.
Thompson, G.R. "Edgar Allan Poe and the Writers of the Old South." *Columbia Literary History of the United States*. Ed. Emory Elliot et al. New York: Columbia UP, 1988. 262-77.
Towner, Theresa M. *The Cambridge Introduction to William Faulkner*. New York: Cambridge UP, 2008.
———. *Faulkner on the Color Line: The Later Novels*. Jackson: UP of Mississippi, 2000.
———. "'It Aint Funny A-Tall': The Transfigured Tales of *The Town*." *Mississippi Quarterly* 44.3 (1991): 321-35.
———. "The Roster, the Chronicle, and the Critic." *Faulkner in the Twenty-First Century: Faulkner and Yoknapatawpha, 2000*. Ed. Robert W. Hamblin and Ann J. Abadie. Jackson: UP of Mississippi, 2003. 1-13.
——— and James B. Carothers. *Reading Faulkner: Collected Stories*. Jackson: UP of Mississippi, 2006.
Trouard, Dawn. "Eula's Plot: An Irigararian Reading of Faulkner's Snopes Trilogy." *Mississippi Quarterly* 42.3 (1989): 281-97.

Urgo, Joseph R. *Faulkner's Apocrypha: A Fable, Snopes, and the Spirit of Human Rebellion*. Jackson: UP of Mississippi, 1989.

———. "*The Reivers*: A Reminiscence." *A William Faulkner Encyclopedia*. Ed. Robert W. Hamblin and Charles A. Peek. Westport: Greenwood Press, 1999. 317-18.

Vickery, Olga W. *The Novels of William Faulkner: A Critical Interpretation*. Baton Rouge: Louisiana State UP, 1964.

Watson, James G. "Literary Self-Criticism: Faulkner in Fiction on Fiction." *Southern Quarterly* 20.1 (1981): 46-63.

Watson, Jay. *Forensic Fictions: The Lawyer Figure in Faulkner*. Athens: U of Georgia P, 1993.

Watson, Ritchie D. "Cavalier." *The Companion to Southern Literature: Themes, Genres, Places, People, Movements, and Motifs*. Ed. Joseph M. Flora, Lucinda H. MacKethan, and Associate Ed. Todd Taylor. Baton Rouge: Louisiana State UP, 2002. 131-33.

———. "Gentleman." *The Companion to Southern Literature: Themes, Genres, Places, People, Movements, and Motifs*. Ed. Joseph M. Flora, Lucinda H. MacKethan, and Associate Ed. Todd Taylor. Baton Rouge: Louisiana State UP, 2002. 292-94.

Weinauer, Ellen. "Romance Genre." *The Companion to Southern Literature: Themes, Genres, Places, People, Movements, and Motifs*. Ed. Joseph M. Flora, Lucinda H. MacKethan, and Associate Ed. Todd Taylor. Baton Rouge: Louisiana State UP, 2002. 744-49.

Williamson, Joel. *William Faulkner and Southern History*. New York: Oxford UP, 1993.

Wilson, Raymond J., III. "Imitative Flem Snopes and Faulkner's Causal Sequence in *The Town*." *Twentieth Century Literature* 26.4 (1980): 432-44.

Wisdom, Joe Craig. *Race and Morality in William Faulkner's Later Novels*. Diss. Florida State U, 1987. Ann Arbor: UMI, 1987. 8805696.

Wittenberg, Judith Bryant. "William Faulkner: A Feminist Consideration." *American Novelists Revisited: Essays in Feminist Criticism*. Ed. Fritz Fleischmann. Boston: G. K. Hall, 1982. 325-38.

Wyatt-Brown, Bertram. *Southern Honor: Ethics and Behavior in the Old South*. New York: Oxford UP, 1982.

Zender, Karl F. *Faulkner and the Politics of Reading*. Baton Rouge: Louisiana State UP, 2002.

———. "*Requiem for a Nun* and the Uses of the Imagination." *Faulkner and Race: Faulkner and Yoknapatawpha 1986*. Ed. Doreen Fowler and Ann J. Abadie. Jackson: UP of Mississippi, 1987. 272-96.

Index

• A •

Adam, 85
American Mercury, 15
Athena, 84

• B •

Banks, Theodore Howard, Jr., 101
Barnes, Djuna, 29, 99 n. 2
Beck, Warren, 75
Betts, Doris, 11
Bleikasten, André, 3, 99 n. 2, 102 n. 5
Blotner, Joseph, 4, 11, 15, 35, 55, 75, 97 n. 2, 98 n. 2, 99 n. 14, 101 n. 2, 102 n. 2, 102 n. 5, 105 n. 18
Bovary, Emma, 73, 106 n. 5
Brinkmeyer, Robert H., Jr., 99 n. 13
Broncano, Manuel, 105 n. 2
Brooks, Cleanth, 38, 58, 63, 64, 65, 73, 97 n. 1, 102 n. 7, 103 n. 12, 108 n. 4
Brown, Calvin S., 57, 103 n. 7
Bulfinch, Thomas, 101 n. 2, 107 n. 10

• C •

Cabell, James Branch, 103 n. 7
Camelot, 60, 107 n. 8
Carmichael, Thomas, 29, 99 n. 1, 99 n. 2
Carothers, James B., 5, 16, 19, 75
Cawelti, John G., 97 n. 4, 97 n. 6
Cerf, Bennett, 25
Cervantes, Miguel de, 56

Chaucer, Geoffrey, 107 n. 13
Chandler, Raymond, 33, 55, 101 n. 18
Clein, Wendy, 70
Cloy, John, 101 n.2
Cobb, James C., 12-13
Cohen, Philip, 3, 70, 103 n. 7
Collins, Carvel, 102 n. 7
Colwell, Frederick A., 74
Commins, Saxe, 39, 49, 74
Cromwell, Oliver, 12

• D •

Davenport, F. Garvin, Jr., 98 n. 5
Davis, Thadious M., 100 n. 3, 101 n.4
Dean, Christopher, 103 n.8
Dixiecrats, 30
Dunlap, Mary Montgomery, 15, 16, 29, 34, 39, 42, 50, 99 n.3
Dussere, Erik, 28, 31

• E •

Ellery Queen's Mystery Magazine, 48, 100 n. 4, 102 n. 4
Erskine, Albert, 93, 108 n. 2
Ettard, Lady, 61
Eve, 85

• F •

Farnsworth, Ann, 105 n. 18
Faulkner, Estelle Oldham, 4, 103 n.7
Faulkner, William
   Characters (except Gavin Stevens):
   Aelia, 57, 62; Allison, Miss, 89; Ames, Dalton, 4; Ballenbaugh, Boyd, 44; Beauchamp, Butch, 17, 20; Beauchamp, Lucas, 22-32 *passim*; Beauchamp, Mollie Worsham (Molly), 17, 20, 22-23, 30, 99 n. 15; Bishop, Eef 107 n. 12; Bookwright, 45-47; Burchett family, 18; Burden, Joanna, 16-17, 98 n.11; Benbow, Horace, 3-4, 13, 15, 98 n. 6, 103 n. 7; Blount, Gavin, 13-15, 98 n. 7; Bundren, Darl, 4; Bundren, Jewel, 4; Christmas, Joe, 17-18, 98 n. 11; Compson, Quentin, 3-4, 56, 71, 98 n. 6; de Spain, Manfred 59-72 *passim*, 89, 103 n. 10, 104 n. 15; Dodge, Granby, 40-41; Dukinfield, Judge, 40; Elys, 57, 62; Farmer, Cecilia, 26-27; Fentry, Jackson, 45-47; Fentry, Jackson and Longstreet (Buck Thorpe), 45-47; Flint, Joel, 48, 49, 101 n. 14; Galwyn, Sir 56-74 *passim*, 103 n. 7; Gombault, Uncle Pete (the marshal), 19-21; Goodyhay, Reverend, 8; Gordon, Charley, 14; the governor ("Monk"), 42-43; Gowrie, Vinson, 23, 25, 28; Grenier, Louis (Lonnie Grinnup), 37, 43-45; Gualdres, Captain (also Gualdes) 1-2, 50-55; Habersham, Miss Eunice, 25; Hampton, Hope, 23, 25; Harker, Otis, 70, 103 n. 11; Harriss, Max, 1-3, 9, 49-51; Harris, Melisandre's unnamed daughter, 2, 49-53, 55; Hightower, Gail, 13, 98 n. 7; Hines, Eupheus (Doc), 17; Hines, Mrs., 17; Hoggenbeck, Boon, 93-94, 108 n. 1, 108 n. 3; Hoggenbeck, Everbe Corinthia (Corrie), 93-94, 108 n. 3; Hoggenbeck, Lucius Priest, 93; Holland, Anse (Virginius's brother in "Smoke"), 41; Holland, Anselm (father in "Smoke"), 41; Holland, Virginius, 40-42; Hood, Uncle Parsham (Possum), 94; Hunger, 57-58, 61-62, 70; Issetibbeha, 76, 108 n. 1; Joe ("Hand Upon the Waters"), 44-45, 101 n. 11; Kohl, Barton, 79; Kohl, Linda Snopes, 18-19, 66-70, 72-73, 78-91 *passim*, 99 n. 12, 103 n. 10, 104 n. 13, 104 n. 14, 104 n. 15, 105 n. 1, 105 n. 2, 105-6 n. 3, 106 n. 4, 106-7 n. 6, 107 n. 8, 107 n. 11, 108 n. 13; Levitt, Matt, 104 n. 15; Little sister Death, 57; Lord of Sleep, 57, 74; Mallison, Charles, Jr. (Chick/Chuck), 14, 22-32 *passim*, 35, 40-42, 45-52, 54-55, 58-59, 61, 67, 68, 71-72, 76, 78-79, 81-82, 86-87, 98 n. 6, 100 n. 12, 101 n. 17, 104 n. 15, 106 n. 3, 106 n. 4, 106 n. 5, 107 n. 9; Mallison, Charles, Sr. (Charley), 81; Mallison, Maggie, 14, 38, 59, 63, 71-72, 82; Mannigoe, Nancy, 6, 15, 22, 35-39, 53-55, 100 n. 3; Maxey, 18; McCallum, Anse, 19, 21; McCallum, Buddy, 19-21; McCallum, Jackson, 20; McCallum, Lucius, 19, 21; McCallum, Old Anse, 19; McCallum, Rafe, 1, 19, 49, 51, 52; McCarron, Hoake, 18, 64, 103 n, 12, 106 n. 4; McCaslin, Isaac 70; McCaslin, Ned, 108 n. 1; Montgomery, Jake, 25; old general (*A Fable*), 7-9; Odlethrop, Stonewall Jackson (Monk), 42-43, 45, 100 n. 4; Otis (*The Reivers*), 93; Pain, 57-58, 61, 70; Pearson, Mr., 19-21; Popeye, 102 n. 3; Priest, Lucius I (Boss, Grandfather), 92-93; Priest, Lucius II, 92-95, 108 n. 1; Priest, Lucius III, 93; Pritchel, Old Man, 48; Pruitt, Mrs., 46; Quick, Isham, 46; Randolph, Lewis, 14-15, 98 n. 9; Ratliff, V.K., 15-16, 18, 58-67, 69, 73, 79-81, 83, 86-89, 90-91, 98 n. 10, 99 n. 12, 103 n. 10, 103 n. 12, 104 n. 13, 104 n. 15, 106 n. 4, 106 n. 5; Reed, Susan, 16, 18-19, 98 n. 10; Rivers, Miss Reba, 102 n. 3; Sander, Aleck 25; Sartoris, Bayard, 4, 106 n. 5; Snopes, Eula Varner, 14, 16, 18, 59, 62-74, 76, 78-85, 91, 99 n. 12, 103 n. 9, 103 n. 10, 103-4 n. 12, 104 n. 13, 104 n. 14, 104 n. 15, 104 n. 16, 106 n. 3, 106 n. 4, 106 n. 5; Snopes, Flem, 18, 58, 60-90 *passim*, 99 n. 12, 105 n. 1, 105 n. 2, 106 n. 3, 106 n. 4, 106 n. 5, 107 n. 12; Snopes, Mink, 80, 84, 86-90, 105 n. 1, 105 n. 2, 106-7 n. 6; Snopes, Montgomery Ward,13, 98 n. 6, 106 n.

• INDEX •

3; St. Francis, 61; Starnes, Sophie, 16-18; Stevens, Gowan, 36, 61, 102 n. 3, 106 n. 4; Stevens, infant daughter of Temple Drake and Gowan, 22; Stevens, Melisandre Backus Harris, 2, 49-53, 55, 67, 81, 107 n. 9; Stevens, Temple Drake, 6, 15-16, 22, 33-34, 37-39, 43, 47, 53-55, 99 n. 2, 99-100 n. 3, 101 n. 16, 102 n. 3; Stribling, Henry (Hawkshaw), 15-16, 18, 98 n. 10; Sutpen, Thomas, 4; Terrel, 42-43; Tristram, Sir, 57, 61, 65; Varner, Mrs., 59; Varner, Will, 47, 59-60; the warden ("Monk"), 42; Worsham, Miss Belle, 17, 20; Yseult, 57, 61-62

Places: Alabama, 16, 18, 26, 75; Beat Four, 27; Division, 16, 18; France, 13, 19, 98 n. 6, 100 n. 13, 101 n. 17; Frenchman's Bend, 45; Greenwich Village, 19, 79, 107 n. 11; Hollywood, 78; Jefferson, 1, 4, 15-16, 19, 25-31 passim, 37, 42, 47-48, 58-59, 66-72 passim, 79-94 passim, 100 n. 6, 104 n. 15, 107 n. 11; Memphis, 1, 9, 13-15, 40, 45, 59, 99 n. 7, 102 n. 3; Mississippi, 11, 15-16, 18, 26, 38, 73, 76, 79, 89, 101 n. 2, 103 n. 12, 105 n. 18; New Orleans, 56; New York, 79, 86, 107 n. 11; Parchman, 80, 87; Pascagoula, 79, 84-85; Red Acres, 11, 97 n. 2; Seminary Hill, 76; Spain, 79; Tennessee, 18; Virginia, 3, 11-12, 18-19, 38, 56, 74, 90, 102 n. 3; West Point, 21; Yoknapatawpha County, 1, 8, 24, 33, 37, 42-43, 58, 76, 79-80, 97 n. 4, 98 n. 11, 100 n. 14, 105 n. 2, 107 n. 11, 108 n. 1

Themes: Cavalier myth, 12-13, 78, 98 n. 3; courtesy, 13, 65, 67, 70, 82-3; courtly love, 3, 65, 69-70, 83-85; curiosity, 14-16, 45-46, 54-55, 87-88; dreams, 36, 56-58, 62, 67, 69, 74, 79, 83, 87, 90-91; faith, 1, 9, 17, 22, 53, 66; freedom, 7, 63, 70, 82, 84, 107 n.11; gaming, 2, 11, 49-50, 54-55, 88-89, 103 n. 7; history, 3, 10-11, 14, 16, 25-27, 29, 31, 47, 77; idealism, 3-5, 8, 13, 29, 37, 43, 56, 59, 65; illusion, 5, 7, 49, 62, 70-71, 74, 86-87, 100 n. 14, 03 n. 7; justice, 3, 8-9, 22-23, 33-55 passim, 59, 79-81, 87, 90, 99 n. 2, 100 n. 7, 105 n. 2; law, 3, 9, 14-15, 19, 23, 33-55 passim, 60, 62-63, 65, 84, 91, 106 n. 3; manipulation, 1-3, 7-9, 15, 33-55 passim, 61-62, 68-69, 81-83, 87, 94, 107 n. 6; myth, 6, 12, 25, 56-77 passim, 84-85, 88, 97 n. 5, 101-2 n. 2, 104 n. 16, 107 n. 10; Old South, 3-4,10-14, 29, 77-78; politics, 5-9, 11-12, 30, 32, 38, 42-43, 74-76, 79, 86, 105 n. 19, 106 n. 3, 107 n. 11; pride, 13, 21, 27, 41, 49, 62, 93; race, 6, 11-12, 15, 17, 23-33 passim, 79, 86, 98 n. 3, 107 n. 11; suicide, 4, 58-59, 70-72, 79-81, 104 n. 14, 104 n. 15, 106 n. 5; truth, 6, 9-11, 14-15, 22, 28, 34, 36-8, 47-8, 52, 54-55, 59, 87, 92, 99 n. 2, 100 n. 7; war, 2, 6-9, 12-15, 19, 21, 27, 30, 50-51, 79-80, 85-86, 89, 105 n. 2, 106 n. 5, 107 n.11; willful innocence, 59, 86-87

Works: *Absalom, Absalom!* 4-5, 98 n. 11; "The Bear,"101 n. 2; "The Big Shot," 98 n. 7; "Dull Tale," 98 n. 7; "An Error in Chemistry," 47-50 passim, 54, 100 n. 4; *Essays, Speeches, and Public Letters*, 75-76; *A Fable*, 6-8, 97 n. 5, 102 n. 5; *Faulkner in the University*, 3, 10-12, 18, 38-39, 56, 74-75, 90-92, 95, 97 n. 1; *Faulkner at West Point*, 21; *Flags in the Dust*, 4, 56, 69, 98 n. 6, 102 n. 5; *Go Down, Moses*, 17, 22-23, 30, 99 n. 4; "Go Down, Moses," 20, 99 n. 14; *The Hamlet*, 104 n.12, 104 n. 16; "Hand Upon the Waters," 37, 44-45, 100 n. 4, 101 n. 15; *Intruder in the Dust*, 14, 22-33 passim, 68, 75-76, 99 n. 3, 100 n. 4; *Knight's Gambit*, 1, 33-55 passim,100 n. 4, 100 n. 5, 101 n. 11, 101 n. 15, 101 n. 17 ; "Knight's Gambit," 1, 9, 49-55, 100 n. 6, 100 n. 7; "Letter to a Northern Editor," 75; *Light in August*, 4, 13, 16-18, 22-23; *Lion in the Garden*, 1, 8, 11, 30, 37, 70, 78, 97 n. 1; *The Mansion*, 8, 18, 54, 59, 62, 66-67, 69, 73, 78-91 passim, 99 n. 12, 102 n. 4, 103 n. 12, 104 n. 13, 105 n. 1, 105 n. 2, 105 n. 19, 106 n. 5, 106 n. 6, 107 n.

11, 107 n. 12; *Mayday*, 55-58, 60-62, 70-72, 74, 101 n. 1, 102 n. 2, 102 n. 4, 102 n. 6, 102-3 n. 7, 104 n. 18; "Monk,"42-43, 45, 100 n. 4; "On Fear: Deep South in Labor: Mississippi," 76; *The Reivers*, 92-95 passim, 108 n. 2, 108 n.3; *Requiem for a Nun*, 6, 8, 9, 15, 22, 26-28, 33-55 passim, 99 n. 2, 100 n. 4, 101 n. 16, 102 n. 3; "A Return," 98 n. 7; "Rose of Lebanon," 13-15, 98 n. 7; *Sanctuary*, 102 n. 3; *Selected Letters*,5, 23-25, 35, 39, 50, 74, 92, 97 n. 2, 98 n. 2, 99 n. 13, 100 n. 13, 102 n. 2, 105 n. 18, 108 n. 2; "Smoke," 15, 40-42, 100 n. 4; *The Sound and the Fury*, 4, 57, 103 n. 7; "The Tall Men," 19-21, 99 n. 13, 99 n. 14; "Tomorrow," 35, 45-47, 100 n. 4; *The Town*, 14, 16, 18, 58-91 passim, 98 n. 6, 99 n. 12, 101 n. 17, 103 n. 11, 103 n. 12, 104 n. 13, 104 n. 15, 105-6 n. 18, 105 n. 19, 106 n. 4, 106 n. 5, 107 n. 9; *William Faulkner Manuscripts 18: Knight's Gambit*, 51-52
Ferguson, James, 20
Fischer, David Hackett, 12
Fisher, Shelia, 104 n. 17
Flannery, M.C., 97 n. 4, 97 n. 6
Folks, Jeffrey J., 97 n. 1
Fulton, Keith Louise, 78, 81, 82, 84, 106 n. 3

• G •

Galatea, 84
Garrett, George, 91
Gawain, Sir, 56-69 passim, 75, 88, 101 n. 1, 101-102 n.2, 102 n. 3, 103 n. 7, 103 n. 8, 103 n. 9, 104 n. 17, 107-08 n. 13
Gollancz, Sir Israel, 101 n. 2
Gordon, E.V., 101-02 n. 2
Green Knight (Bertilak), 56, 60-72 passim, 88, 101 n. 2, 103 n. 7, 103 n. 9, 104 n. 17, 107 n. 13
Gregory, Eileen, 105 n. 19
Grenier, Cynthia, 70
Gromer, Sir, 107 n. 13
Guinevere, 61, 65, 72, 107 n. 8

• H •

Haas, Robert K., 23, 24, 92, 99 n. 13
Hagood, Taylor,101 n. 1
Hamblin, Robert W., 99 n. 3
Hanaoka, Shigeru, 103 n. 7
Harley, Marta Powell, 56, 63, 101 n.1, 101 n. 2, 103 n.7, 103 n.9
Harper's Bazaar, 15, 35, 100 n. 4
Hautdesert, Lady of, 61-71 passim, 104 n. 17
Helen of Troy, 65, 90
Hönnighausen, Lothar, 97 n.1
Howe, Irving, 34
Howe, Russell, 11

• I •

Irwin, John T., 4, 50, 97 n. 1, 98 n. 6, 100 n.6, 101 n. 18
Isolde, 65

• J •

Jebb, John F., 35, 37, 38, 42, 46, 99 n. 1, 100 n. 7, 100 n. 8
Jonsson, Else, 5
Juliet, 65, 85

• K •

Kang, Hee, 79, 105-6 n.3
Karaganis, Joe, 6
Karl, Frederick R., 100 n. 5
Kartiganer, Donald, 14
King James Bible, 44
Klinkowitz, Jerome F., 45, 100 n. 6
Kulseth, Leonard I., 38

• L •

Ladd, Barbara, 33-34, 99 n. 1
Launcelot, 65, 72, 107 n. 8

le Fay, Morgan, 60, 61
Levitsky, Holli G., 72, 106 n. 5
Longley, John Lewis, Jr., 34, 72
Lyman, Helen Baird, 56, 102-3 n. 7, 104-5 n. 18

• M •

Malory, Sir Thomas, 60, 62, 72
Marlowe, Philip, 33, 55
Marx, Charles A., 38
Matthews, John T., 21, 99 n. 13, 107 n. 11
McHaney, Thomas L., 100 n. 4
McMillen, Neil R., 11
Meats, Stephen E., 17, 98 n. 11
Meindl, Dieter, 13, 98 n. 9
Meriwether, James B., 15
A Midsummer Night's Dream, 85
Millgate, Michael, 33, 35-36, 40, 93, 98 n.7, 99 n.2
Milum, Richard A., 98 n. 4
Monaghan, David M., 4
Moreland, Richard C., 22, 31
Morrison, Gail Moore, 103 n. 7
"My Last Duchess," 73

• N •

Norris, Nancy, 85

• O •

Ober, Harold, 100 n. 13
Ovid, 85

• P •

Paris, 65
Payne, Thomas E., 38
Pearl, 102 n. 2
Pelleas, Sir, 61
Polk, Noel, 5-8, 11, 34, 37, 68, 75, 97 n. 5, 99 n. 1, 99 n. 2, 102 n. 4, 107 n. 7

Pygmalion, 84
Pyramus, 85, 107 n. 10

• Q •

Quixote, Don, 18, 56

• R •

Ragnelle, Dame, 88, 107-8 n. 13
Random House, 23, 35, 74, 93, 107 n. 7
Reames, Kelly Lynch, 99 n. 2
Roberts, Diane, 53, 78, 84, 99 n. 2
Romeo, 65, 85
Romeo and Juliet, 85
Rubin, Louis D., Jr., 4, 97 n. 1

• S •

Salda, Michael N., 57-58, 60-61, 70, 101 n. 1, 102 n. 6, 103 n. 7
Samway, Patrick, S.J., 2, 24-25, 44
Saturday Evening Post, The, 100 n. 4
Sayre, Robert Woods, 13, 98 n. 7
Schlepper, W.E., 36-37, 50, 100 n. 7, 101 n. 18
Scribner's Magazine, 100 n. 4
Semiramis, 72, 85, 107 n. 10
Shakespeare, William, 85
Simpson, Lewis P., 97 n. 1
Sir Gawain and the Green Knight, 56, 60-75 passim, 88, 101 n.1, 101-2 n. 2, 102 n. 3, 103 n. 7, 103 n. 8, 103 n. 9, 104 n. 17, 107-8 n. 13
Skei, Hans H., 38, 98 n. 10, 100 n. 12, 100 n. 14
Spanish Civil War, 79, 106 n. 2
Stein, Jean, 105 n. 18
Sternwood, Carmen, 55
Stone, Phil, 75
Stroble, Woodrow, 58, 90

• T •

Tangum, Marion, 3
Taylor, William R., 12
Thiabe, 85, 107 n. 10
Thompson, G.R., 98 n. 4
Tolkien, Christopher, 102 n. 2
Tolkien, J.R.R., 101-2 n. 2
Towner, Theresa M., 5-6, 16, 19, 26, 59, 75, 102 n. 4, 105 n. 21
Trouard, Dawn, 63, 73, 104 n. 16

• U •

University of Virginia, 3, 11, 18, 38, 56, 74, 90
Urgo, Joseph R., 5-7, 59, 75, 87, 93, 97 n. 5, 105 n. 20

• V •

Vickery, Olga W., 33, 37, 94, 108 n. 1

• W •

Watson, James G., 103 n. 7
Watson, Jay, 16, 18, 23-24, 104 n. 14
Watson, Ritchie D., 12-13
Weinauer, Ellen, 98 n. 4
Weston, Jessie L., 101 n. 2
Wife of Bath, 107 n. 13
Williams, Joan, 35
Williamson, Joel, 10
Wilson, Raymond J., III., 104 n. 14
Wisdom, Joe Craig, 6-7
Wisdom, William B., 56-7, 102 n. 6
Wittenberg, Judith Bryant, 8
Wyatt-Brown, Bertram, 13

• Z •

Zender, Karl F., 6, 8, 34

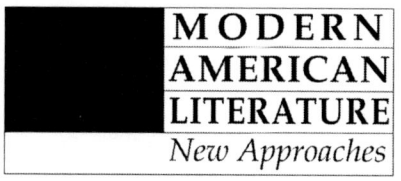
MODERN AMERICAN LITERATURE
New Approaches

Yoshinobu Hakutani, *General Editor*

The books in this series deal with many of the major writers known as American realists, modernists, and post-modernists from 1880 to the present. This category of writers will also include less known ethnic and minority writers, a majority of whom are African American, some are Native American, Mexican American, Japanese American, Chinese American, and others. The series might also include studies on well-known contemporary writers, such as James Dickey, Allen Ginsberg, Gary Snyder, John Barth, John Updike, and Joyce Carol Oates. In general, the series will reflect new critical approaches such as deconstructionism, new historicism, psychoanalytical criticism, gender criticism/feminism, and cultural criticism.

For additional information about this series or for the submission of manuscripts, please contact:

> Peter Lang Publishing
> P.O. Box 1246
> Bel Air, MD 21014-1246

To order other books in this series, please contact our Customer Service Department at:

> 800-770-LANG (within the U.S.)
> (212) 647-7706 (outside the U.S.)
> (212) 647-7707 FAX

Or browse online by series at:

> www.peterlang.com